GOODSON MUMBA

The Global Economics

Navigating Public Finance and International Trade

Copyright © 2024 by Goodson Mumba

All rights reserved. No part of this publication may be reproduced, stored or transmitted in any form or by any means, electronic, mechanical, photocopying, recording, scanning, or otherwise without written permission from the publisher. It is illegal to copy this book, post it to a website, or distribute it by any other means without permission.

First edition

ISBN: 9798335038294

This book was professionally typeset on Reedsy. Find out more at reedsy.com

Contents

Preface	viii
Acknowledgement	xi
Dedication	xii
Disclaimer	xiii
1 Chapter 1: Introduction to Global Economics	1
1.1 Understanding Economic Interdependence	1
1.2 The Role of Public Finance in Global Economics	3
1.3 The Impact of International Trade on National Economies	6
1.4 Historical Perspectives on Global Economic Integration	8
1.5 Challenges and Opportunities in the Global Economic Landscape	11
1.6 Key Concepts and Terminology in Global Economics	13
2 Chapter 2: Foundations of Public Finance	16
2.1 Principles of Taxation and Revenue Generation	16
2.2 Government Budgeting and Fiscal Policy	18
2.3 Public Expenditure Management	20
2.4 Debt Management Strategies	22
2.5 Financial Institutions and Markets	24
2.6 Economic Development Planning and Policy Formulation	26

3 Chapter 3: The Dynamics of International Trade 29
  3.1 Trade Theories and Comparative Advantage 29
  3.2 Trade Policies and Tariff Structures 31
  3.3 Trade Agreements and Regional Integration 33
  3.4 Foreign Direct Investment (FDI) and Multinational Corporations 35
  3.5 Exchange Rates and Currency Markets 37
  3.6 Trade Facilitation and Supply Chain Management 39
4 Chapter 4: Macroeconomic Policy Coordination 42
  4.1 Monetary Policy and Central Banking 42
  4.2 Exchange Rate Regimes and Policy Options 44
  4.3 Inflation Targeting and Price Stability 46
  4.4 Coordination of Fiscal and Monetary Policies 48
  4.5 Global Economic Governance and Institutions 50
  4.5 Global Economic Governance and Institutions 52
  4.6 Crisis Management and Economic Resilience Strategies 54
5 Chapter 5: Trade and Development 57
  5.1 Trade and Sustainable Development Goals (SDGs) 57
  5.2 Trade-Related Aspects of Intellectual Property Rights 59

5.3 Trade and Environmental Sustainability 61
5.4 Trade, Gender, and Social Inclusion 63
5.5 Trade and Poverty Alleviation Strategies 65
5.6 Trade and Human Rights Considerations 67

6 Chapter 6: International Financial Architecture 70
6.1 The Role of International Financial Institutions (IFIs) 70
6.2 International Monetary Fund (IMF) Programs and Conditionality 72
6.3 World Bank Group Initiatives and Development Financing 74
6.4 Regional Development Banks and Financial Assistance 76
6.5 Sovereign Debt Restructuring and Debt Relief Initiatives 78
6.6 Emerging Trends in Global Financial Governance 80

7 Chapter 7: Trade Policy Analysis and Evaluation 83
7.1 Quantitative Methods in Trade Policy Analysis 83
7.2 Trade Policy Instruments and Their Effects 85
7.3 Trade Liberalization and Economic Growth 87
7.4 Impact Assessment of Trade Agreements 90
7.5 Trade Dispute Resolution Mechanisms 92

	7.6 Trade Policy Formulation and Implementation Challenges	95
8	Chapter 8: Public Finance in Global Context	98
	8.1 International Taxation and Tax Harmonization	98
	8.2 Cross-Border Financial Flows and Capital Controls	100
	8.3 Public-Private Partnerships (PPPs) in Infrastructure Development	103
	8.4 Sovereign Wealth Funds and Resource Management	106
	8.5 Global Economic Crises and Contagion Effects	108
	8.6; Fiscal Federalization and Subnational Governance in a Globalized Economy	111
9	Chapter 9: Trade and Technology	114
	9.1 Digital Trade and E-Commerce Regulations	114
	9.2 Innovation Policies and Technological Development	117
	9.3 Trade in Services and Mode 4 Movement of Persons	119
	9.4 Intellectual Property Rights (IPR) Protection and Enforcement	122
	9.5 Artificial Intelligence (AI) and the Future of Trade	125
	9.6 Blockchain Technology and Trade Finance Innovation	128
10	Chapter 10: Regional Economic Integration Models and Lessons	131
	10.1 European Union (EU) Integration Models and Lessons Learned	131

10.2 African Continental Free Trade Area (AfCFTA) Implementation	134
10.3 Asia-Pacific Economic Cooperation (APEC) and Regional Cooperation	137
10.4 Mercosur and South American Integration Efforts	140
10.5 Economic Community of West African States (ECOWAS) Regional Integration	142
10.6 Association of Southeast Asian Nations (ASEAN) Economic Integration Initiatives	145
About the Author	148

Preface

As a researcher and engaged citizen of Zambia, I have followed our country's economic journey with keen interest and a critical eye. Zambia, like many nations, has navigated the turbulent waters of global economics, striving for growth, stability, and development. My passion for understanding the intricacies of public finance and international trade has driven me to explore these topics deeply, culminating in the creation of "Global Economics Navigating Public Finance and International Trade."

This book is a product of years of research, observation, and analysis of Zambia's economic policies and their interactions with global markets. It aims to provide readers with a comprehensive understanding of the essential principles of public finance and international trade, illustrated through the lens of Zambia's experiences and broader global contexts.

The journey begins with an exploration of economic interdependence, highlighting how interconnected our world has become. Understanding these connections is crucial for appreciating the broader impacts of national economic policies and international trade agreements. This foundation sets the stage for delving into the specifics of public finance, including taxation, budgeting, and expenditure management. These principles are vital for comprehending how governments fund their operations and drive development.

The chapters dedicated to international trade provide an in-depth look at trade theories, policies, and agreements. By examining how different countries navigate the complexities of global trade, we gain valuable insights into the strategies that promote economic growth and the challenges that must be overcome.

Throughout the book, I have incorporated practical examples and case studies from various regions, including Zambia. These real-world scenarios illustrate the successes and lessons learned, offering a well-rounded perspective on global economic practices. One of the core themes is the importance of regional economic integration. By exploring initiatives such as the European Union, the African Continental Free Trade Area, and ASEAN, we see how regional cooperation can enhance economic stability and growth.

The sections on international financial architecture and trade policy analysis further enrich the discussion, providing a deep understanding of the institutions and instruments that shape global economic governance. From the role of international financial institutions to the intricacies of trade policy evaluation, these chapters equip readers with the tools to critically assess and engage with global economic issues.

My gratitude extends to the many economists, policymakers, academics, and colleagues who have contributed their expertise and perspectives. Their insights have been invaluable in shaping the content of this book. Special thanks are due to my research team, whose dedication and hard work have been crucial in bringing this project to fruition.

"Global Economics Navigating Public Finance and International Trade" is intended for a diverse audience, including students, policymakers, business leaders, and anyone interested in understanding the forces that drive the global economy. It is my hope that this book will serve as a valuable resource, fostering informed discussions and inspiring innovative solutions to the economic challenges we face today.

As we embark on this journey through the complexities of global economics, I invite you to explore the interconnected world of public finance and international trade. Together, we can navigate these intricacies and contribute to a more prosperous and stable global economy.

Sincerely,

Goodson Mumba

Acknowledgement

I would like to eternally and gratefully acknowledge the Almighty God for the infinite intelligence from His universal mind where we draw from all that we come to know and are yet to know. May I also acknowledge and thank everyone that has played a part in my journey of life in terms of spiritual, moral, emotional and material support.

Dedication

I extend my sincerest gratitude to my beloved wife, Edith Mumba, and our children, Angelina, Lubuto, Letticia, Lulumbi, and Butusho, for their unwavering support and understanding throughout the conception, writing, and eventual publication of this book, despite the sacrifices and challenges they endured.

Disclaimer

This book is a work of fiction. Names, characters, businesses, places, events, and incidents are either the products of the author's imagination or used in a fictitious manner. Any resemblance to actual persons, living or dead, or actual events is purely coincidental.

1

Chapter 1: Introduction to Global Economics

1.1 Understanding Economic Interdependence

In a high-ceilinged conference room at the Ministry of Finance in Lusaka, Minister Peter Lumamba opened the meeting with a solemn yet determined tone. He acknowledged the challenges ahead and stressed the importance of understanding economic interdependence as the team embarked on their mission to navigate global economics.

"Today marks the beginning of a crucial journey," he began, his voice resonating with a mix of urgency and optimism. He explained that their goal was to master the complexities of global economics and steer Zambia toward sustainable growth.

Director Chisala took the floor next, outlining the concept of economic interdependence. "Our trade with other nations," he stated, "is not just about exporting copper or importing technology. It's about how these transactions weave into the larger economic fabric." He described how the mutual reliance between economies globally influenced local conditions and how a shift in demand or policy in one part of the world could have significant repercussions in Zambia.

The narrative then shifted to a mining town in the Copperbelt Province, where copper, Zambia's primary export, was being extracted. Miners worked diligently, and trucks loaded with ore headed to processing plants, eventually reaching ships at port ready to transport the copper overseas. Director Chisala's voiceover illustrated that the value of copper was determined by markets thousands of miles away, emphasizing the delicate balance of global supply and demand.

The scene moved to Brussels, where Zambian trade delegates were negotiating a new trade agreement with the European Union. The negotiations were intense, each side presenting their terms. A Zambian delegate highlighted the importance of access to European markets for Zambia's growth, proposing reduced tariffs on copper in exchange for lower barriers on European machinery imports. The European delegate countered, seeking assurances on environmental standards and sustainable mining practices.

Director Chisala's voiceover returned, explaining that these negotiations were a vivid example of economic interdependence in action. He stressed that trade agreements could open new opportunities but also bring new responsibilities.

Back in Lusaka, at the Ministry of Finance, Minister Lumamba and his team watched a live feed of the negotiations. The tension in the room was palpable as they witnessed the economic interdependence unfold in real-time. Minister Lumamba reflected on the significance of these international agreements, asking Director Patel about their implications for Zambia's fiscal policies.

Director Patel leaned forward and explained, "We must align our fiscal policies with global standards. This means investing in sustainable practices and diversifying our economy to support our international commitments."

The story then moved to a rural community in Zambia, where agricultural development projects, funded by international aid and trade partnerships, were underway. Farmers were learning new techniques to increase yield and sustainability. Director Patel's voiceover illustrated how global interdependence impacted local development, bringing in resources and knowledge that drove progress.

The narrative returned to the conference room at the Ministry of Finance. The directors, now engaged in animated discussions, shared ideas freely. Minister Lumamba observed them thoughtfully, emphasizing that their task was to navigate this complex web with wisdom and foresight. "Together, we can turn interdependence into a strength for Zambia," he concluded.

The chapter closed with a panoramic view of the vibrant energy in the room, setting the stage for the challenges and triumphs to come in their journey through global economics.

1.2 The Role of Public Finance in Global Economics

Following the previous discussion on economic interdependence, Minister Peter Lumamba stood at the head of the table, ready to delve into the next crucial topic the role of public finance in global economics. He looked around the room, his gaze steady and determined.

"Understanding interdependence is only the beginning," Minister Lumamba began. "Now, we must explore how public finance shapes and is shaped by global economics. Director Tembo, could you lead us through this?"

Director Tembo, a seasoned expert in fiscal policy, rose to address the team. "Public finance," he explained, "encompasses the revenue collection and expenditure by the government. Its role in global economics is profound. Let me illustrate with a few examples."

The scene shifted to the bustling Lusaka Stock Exchange, where traders were engrossed in their work. The hum of activity underscored Director Tembo's voiceover.

"Our budgetary decisions impact investor confidence," he continued. "For instance, when we implement sound fiscal policies, it attracts foreign investment, which in turn strengthens our currency and boosts economic growth."

The narrative moved to a rural school, newly built and buzzing with eager children. This school was a product of public finance, funded through careful allocation of national revenue.

"Public finance isn't just about balancing books," Director Tembo's voiceover continued. "It's about investing in our future—education, healthcare, and infrastructure. These investments create a more robust, skilled workforce that can compete globally."

The story shifted to an international economic forum, where Zambia's fiscal policies were being scrutinized by international financial institutions and potential investors. Minister Lumamba and Director Tembo were present, engaging in discussions and negotiations.

"Public finance also involves navigating the scrutiny of global economic watchdogs," Tembo explained. "Our fiscal health is constantly monitored by institutions like the IMF and World

Bank. Their assessments influence our credit ratings and access to international financing."

Back in Lusaka, Minister Lumamba and his team met with representatives from the International Monetary Fund. The discussions were intense, focusing on fiscal reforms and economic strategies.

"We need to align our policies with international standards," an IMF representative advised. "This will help stabilize your economy and build investor confidence."

"Balancing our budget isn't just a domestic issue; it's a global one. The policies we adopt must resonate with international expectations while addressing local needs."

The camera returned to the conference room at the Ministry of Finance. The directors were now fully immersed in understanding the complexities of public finance in a global context. Director Patel, reflecting on the earlier discussions, spoke up.

"Our fiscal policies must support sustainable growth," he said. "This means reducing our dependency on volatile markets and investing in sectors that ensure long-term stability."

Minister Lumamba nodded, adding, "We also need to address debt management. Sustainable borrowing and efficient use of funds are crucial to maintaining our economic sovereignty."

The directors resumed their discussions, brainstorming strategies to enhance Zambia's fiscal policies in line with global economic standards. The room buzzed with ideas and energy, each member contributing their expertise.

Minister Lumamba looked around the room, a sense of pride and determination evident on his face. "We have a clear understanding of our role in the global economic landscape. Let's leverage our public finance to build a resilient and prosperous Zambia."

The camera panned out, capturing the dynamic atmosphere as the team dove deeper into their mission. The foundation was set, and the journey through the intricacies of global economics and public finance had truly begun.

1.3 The Impact of International Trade on National Economies

The room at the Ministry of Finance was filled with anticipation as Minister Peter Lumamba introduced the next topic. "Now that we've covered economic interdependence and the role of public finance, let's delve into how international trade impacts our national economy. Director Mwila, please lead us through this discussion."

Director Mwila, known for her expertise in trade policy, stood and addressed the team. "International trade," she began, "is a double-edged sword. It can drive growth and development, but it also comes with challenges. Let's explore both sides."

The scene shifted to the bustling Port of Dar es Salaam, where Zambian goods were being loaded onto ships bound for various international markets. Workers moved efficiently, and cranes swung containers into place with rhythmic precision.

Director Mwila's voiceover explained, "Our exports, such as copper, agricultural products, and gemstones, are vital to our economy. Trade opens up new markets, driving revenue and creating jobs. But it's a complex equation."

The narrative moved to a modern textile factory in Lusaka, where workers were busy at their machines, producing garments for export. The scene highlighted the growth of local industries spurred by international trade agreements.

"International trade also fosters industrial growth," Mwila

continued. "By tapping into global markets, we attract investments and stimulate domestic production. This creates a ripple effect, boosting ancillary industries and services."

The story then transitioned to a vibrant rural market, where imported goods from various countries were sold alongside local produce. The bustling market showcased the variety of products available to Zambian consumers, from electronics to textiles.

"But there's a downside," Mwila's voiceover cautioned. "Increased imports can outcompete local businesses, leading to job losses and economic displacement. We must balance opening our markets with protecting domestic industries."

The scene shifted to a high-stakes trade negotiation between Zambian officials and a delegation from China. The room was tense as both sides worked to finalize a trade deal that would increase Zambian exports in exchange for Chinese technology and infrastructure investments.

"Negotiations are key," Mwila explained. "We need favorable trade terms to ensure our economy benefits. This means securing deals that open markets for our exports while gaining access to vital technology and investment."

The narrative moved to a small business in Zambia that had flourished due to increased trade opportunities. The owner, a young entrepreneur, spoke about how international demand for her handcrafted goods had transformed her business.

"Trade empowers entrepreneurs," Mwila's voiceover noted. "It provides access to new markets and opportunities for innovation and growth. Small businesses can scale up and become significant players in the economy."

Back at the Ministry of Finance, the directors were deeply engaged in a lively discussion about the impacts of international trade. Director Chisala pointed out the importance of trade policy alignment, while Director Patel emphasized the need for strategic investments in competitive sectors.

Minister Lumamba, summarizing the discussions, said, "International trade is indeed a powerful tool for economic growth. However, we must be vigilant and strategic in our approach. Protecting our industries, securing fair trade deals, and fostering innovation are crucial."

He looked around the room, his expression resolute. "Our goal is to harness the benefits of international trade while mitigating its risks. By doing so, we can build a resilient and prosperous economy."

The camera panned out, capturing the directors' determined faces and the collaborative energy in the room. The discussion on international trade had laid the groundwork for understanding its profound impact on Zambia's national economy, setting the stage for future strategies and decisions.

1.4 Historical Perspectives on Global Economic Integration

As the discussion on the impact of international trade concluded, Minister Peter Lumamba shifted the focus to historical perspectives on global economic integration. The room was filled with anticipation as Director Banda, a renowned economist, prepared to share insights into the topic.

"Understanding the historical context of global economic integration is essential for navigating the present landscape," Minister Lumamba emphasized, setting the tone for the discussion.

The scene shifted to the Copperbelt region in the 19th

century, where British colonialists established mines to extract copper. The landscape was dotted with mining camps, and local communities were drawn into the global economy through labor and trade.

Director Banda's voiceover explained, "The colonial era marked the beginning of Zambia's integration into the global economy. The demand for copper fueled industrialization in Europe, while local communities experienced profound social and economic changes."

The narrative moved to Zambia's independence era in the 1960s, with scenes of jubilant crowds celebrating freedom from colonial rule. Newly independent nations sought to assert their sovereignty on the global stage and chart their economic destinies.

"The post-independence period saw a wave of economic nationalism," Director Banda continued. "Zambia, under President Kenneth Kaunda's leadership, pursued policies of import substitution and nationalization to build domestic industries and reduce dependency on foreign imports."

The story then transitioned to the tumultuous era of the 1980s, marked by economic crises and structural adjustment programs imposed by international financial institutions. Scenes of protests and austerity measures underscored the challenges faced by Zambia and other developing nations.

"The 1980s ushered in a new era of globalization," Director Banda explained. "Structural adjustment programs promoted liberalization, privatization, and deregulation, aiming to integrate developing economies into the global market."

The narrative fast-forwarded to the new millennium, with scenes of technological advancements, global trade agreements, and the rise of emerging economies. Zambia, like many nations, grappled with the opportunities and challenges of a rapidly evolving global economy.

"In the 21st century, globalization accelerated," Director Banda's voiceover noted. "Advancements in technology and communication reshaped global supply chains, facilitating trade and investment on an unprecedented scale. Zambia's economy became increasingly intertwined with the global market."

Back at the Ministry of Finance, the directors listened intently as Director Banda concluded his historical overview. The room was filled with a sense of reflection and understanding as they grasped the complexities of Zambia's journey in the global economic landscape.

Minister Lumamba, acknowledging the significance of historical perspectives, said, "Our past informs our present. By understanding the forces that have shaped our economy, we can better navigate the challenges and opportunities of the future."

The camera panned out, capturing the directors deep in thought, contemplating the lessons of history and their implications for Zambia's economic trajectory. The discussion on historical perspectives had provided valuable insights, laying the groundwork for informed decision-making in the dynamic world of global economics.

1.5 Challenges and Opportunities in the Global Economic Landscape

After reflecting on historical perspectives, Minister Peter Lumamba turned the discussion to the present challenges and opportunities in the global economic landscape. The atmosphere in the room was focused yet tinged with anticipation as Director Sibanda, an expert in international economics, prepared to share insights.

"Understanding the current landscape is crucial for navigating the complexities of global economics," Minister Lumamba emphasized, setting the stage for the discussion.

The scene transitioned to a montage of news reports from various parts of the world, highlighting global economic trends and challenges. Reports of trade tensions, currency fluctuations, and geopolitical conflicts underscored the volatility of the global economic landscape.

Director Sibanda's voiceover explained, "The global economic landscape is characterized by both challenges and opportunities. Rapid technological advancements, shifting trade patterns, and geopolitical tensions pose significant challenges, while globalization and interconnectedness offer unprecedented opportunities."

The narrative moved to a trade negotiation room in Geneva, where delegates from different countries engaged in heated discussions over trade barriers and tariffs. The atmosphere was tense as negotiators sought to protect their national interests while navigating complex trade dynamics.

"Trade negotiations are fraught with challenges," Director Sibanda continued. "Divergent interests, protectionist policies, and regulatory barriers often hinder progress. However, successful negotiations can lead to mutually beneficial outcomes and open new avenues for economic cooperation."

The story then transitioned to a bustling technological innovation hub in Silicon Valley, where entrepreneurs and researchers worked tirelessly on cutting-edge technologies. Scenes of innovation and collaboration highlighted the transformative power of technology in shaping the global economy.

"Technological innovation presents both challenges and opportunities," Director Sibanda noted. "While automation and digitization may disrupt traditional industries and job markets, they also drive productivity gains and create new economic sectors, fostering innovation and growth."

The narrative shifted to a climate change summit in Paris, where world leaders gathered to discuss strategies for combating climate change and transitioning to a sustainable economy. The urgency of addressing environmental challenges underscored the interconnectedness of economic, social, and environmental factors.

"Climate change poses significant challenges to the global economy," Director Sibanda explained. "Rising sea levels, extreme weather events, and resource scarcity threaten economic stability and growth. However, transitioning to a low-carbon economy presents opportunities for green investments, job creation, and sustainable development."

Back at the Ministry of Finance, the directors absorbed the insights shared by Director Sibanda. The room was filled with a sense of urgency and determination as they contemplated the challenges and opportunities that lay ahead in the global economic landscape.

Minister Lumamba, acknowledging the complexities of the present landscape, said, "In navigating the global economic landscape, we must remain vigilant and adaptable. By addressing challenges head-on and seizing opportunities, we can chart a course towards sustainable growth and prosperity for Zambia."

The camera panned out, capturing the directors deep in discussion, strategizing ways to navigate the challenges and leverage the opportunities in the dynamic world of global economics. The discussion on challenges and opportunities had provided valuable insights, equipping them to make informed decisions in shaping Zambia's economic future.

1.6 Key Concepts and Terminology in Global Economics

As the discussion on challenges and opportunities in the global economic landscape concluded, Minister Peter Lumamba shifted the focus to understanding key concepts and terminology. The room was abuzz with anticipation as Director Ngoma, an esteemed economist, prepared to share insights into the intricacies of global economics.

"Understanding the key concepts and terminology is essential for navigating the complexities of global economics," Minister Lumamba emphasized, setting the stage for the discussion.

The scene transitioned to a classroom setting, where Director Ngoma stood at the front, ready to impart knowledge to eager students. Charts and graphs adorned the walls, illustrating economic theories and principles.

"Global economics is a vast field encompassing various concepts and terminology," Director Ngoma began. "From supply and demand to exchange rates and trade policies, these concepts form the foundation of our understanding of the global economy."

The narrative moved to a bustling stock exchange trading floor, where traders shouted orders and monitored fluctuating stock prices. Director Ngoma's voiceover explained the intricacies of financial markets and investment strategies.

"Financial markets play a crucial role in the global economy," Director Ngoma continued. "Understanding concepts such as stocks, bonds, and derivatives is essential for analyzing market trends and making informed investment decisions."

The story then transitioned to a trade negotiation room, where diplomats engaged in discussions over trade agreements and tariffs. Director Ngoma's voiceover elucidated the complexities of trade policies and their impact on international commerce.

"Trade policies shape the flow of goods and services across borders," Director Ngoma explained. "Concepts such as tariffs, quotas, and trade agreements determine the terms of trade between nations, influencing economic growth and development."

The narrative shifted to a meeting of central bankers, where policymakers discussed monetary policies and interest rates. Director Ngoma's voiceover delved into the role of central banks in managing inflation and stabilizing the economy.

"Monetary policy is a powerful tool for central banks to influence economic activity," Director Ngoma noted. "Key concepts such as interest rates, money supply, and inflation targeting guide policymakers in achieving price stability and sustainable growth."

Back at the Ministry of Finance, the directors absorbed the insights shared by Director Ngoma. The room was filled with a sense of enlightenment as they deepened their understanding of key concepts and terminology in global economics.

Minister Lumamba, acknowledging the importance of knowledge and education, said, "In mastering the key concepts and terminology, we equip ourselves with the tools to navigate the complexities of the global economy. Let us continue to learn and grow, as we work towards building a prosperous future for Zambia."

The camera panned out, capturing the directors engaged in lively discussions, eager to apply their newfound understanding in shaping Zambia's economic policies. The discussion on key concepts and terminology had provided invaluable insights, empowering them to make informed decisions in the dynamic world of global economics.

Chapter 2: Foundations of Public Finance

2.1 Principles of Taxation and Revenue Generation

Minister Peter Lumamba convened the next meeting, focusing on the principles of taxation and revenue generation. The room buzzed with anticipation as Director Mulenga, a seasoned economist, prepared to delve into the intricacies of tax policy.

"Taxation is the cornerstone of public finance," Minister Lumamba began, emphasizing its importance. "Director Mulenga, please enlighten us on the principles guiding taxation and revenue generation."

The scene transitioned to a classroom setting within the Ministry of Finance, where Director Mulenga stood at the front, ready to impart knowledge to his attentive audience. Charts and diagrams adorned the walls, illustrating various tax structures and revenue streams.

"Taxation serves multiple purposes in public finance," Director Mulenga began. "It not only raises revenue for government expenditures but also promotes economic stability, equity, and efficiency."

The narrative shifted to a bustling market square in Lusaka, where vendors sold their goods amid the hustle and bustle of daily life. Director Mulenga's voiceover elucidated the concept of tax equity and fairness.

"Equity in taxation means that the burden should be distributed fairly among taxpayers based on their ability to pay," Director Mulenga explained. "Policies such as progressive taxation ensure that those with higher incomes contribute a larger proportion of their earnings."

The story then transitioned to a small business owner's shop, where he meticulously managed his finances. Director Mulenga's voiceover continued, discussing the principles of tax efficiency and simplicity.

"Tax systems should be designed to minimize administrative costs and compliance burdens," Director Mulenga noted. "Simplicity and efficiency in tax administration promote economic growth and reduce the risk of tax evasion."

Back at the Ministry of Finance, the directors absorbed the insights shared by Director Mulenga. The room was filled with a sense of enlightenment as they deepened their understanding of tax policy principles.

Minister Lumamba, acknowledging the importance of taxation in public finance, said, "Taxation is a powerful tool for government revenue generation and economic management. Let us apply these principles wisely as we chart a course towards fiscal sustainability and prosperity for Zambia."

The camera panned out, capturing the directors engaged in lively discussions, eager to apply their newfound understanding in shaping Zambia's tax policies. The discussion on the principles of taxation and revenue generation had provided invaluable insights, empowering them to make informed decisions in the realm of public finance.

2.2 Government Budgeting and Fiscal Policy

Following the discussion on taxation principles, Minister Peter Lumamba shifted the focus to government budgeting and fiscal policy. The room was filled with anticipation as Director Tembo, a seasoned economist, prepared to share insights into the intricacies of fiscal management.

"Government budgeting and fiscal policy are essential tools for shaping economic outcomes," Minister Lumamba began, emphasizing their significance. "Director Tembo, please enlighten us on the principles guiding budget formulation and fiscal policy."

The scene transitioned to a budget planning meeting within the Ministry of Finance, where Director Tembo led a team of economists and policymakers through the intricacies of budget formulation. Charts and graphs adorned the walls, illustrating revenue projections and expenditure priorities.

"Government budgeting involves allocating scarce resources to meet the needs and priorities of society," Director Tembo explained, addressing his attentive audience. "It encompasses revenue generation, expenditure planning, and debt management."

The narrative shifted to a rural community meeting, where government officials engaged with local residents to discuss development priorities. Director Tembo's voiceover elucidated the role of fiscal policy in promoting economic stability and growth.

"Fiscal policy refers to the use of government spending and taxation to influence economic outcomes," Director Tembo noted. "During times of economic downturn, expansionary fiscal policies such as increased government spending and tax cuts can stimulate demand and promote growth."

The story then transitioned to a meeting between Zambian government officials and representatives from international financial institutions. The discussions centered on fiscal reforms and strategies to address budget deficits and debt sustainability.

"Fiscal discipline is crucial for maintaining macroeconomic stability," Director Tembo emphasized, addressing the importance of prudent fiscal management. "Sound fiscal policies, including budget deficit targets and debt sustainability frameworks, are essential for safeguarding the country's financial health."

Back at the Ministry of Finance, the directors absorbed the insights shared by Director Tembo. The room was filled with a sense of enlightenment as they deepened their understanding of budgeting principles and fiscal policy.

Minister Lumamba, acknowledging the importance of fiscal management, said, "Government budgeting and fiscal policy play a pivotal role in promoting economic development and ensuring fiscal sustainability. Let us apply these principles judiciously as we strive to build a prosperous future for Zambia."

The camera panned out, capturing the directors engaged in lively discussions, eager to apply their newfound understanding in shaping Zambia's fiscal policies. The discussion on government budgeting and fiscal policy had provided invaluable insights, empowering them to make informed decisions in the realm of public finance.

2.3 Public Expenditure Management

After discussing government budgeting and fiscal policy, Minister Peter Lumamba directed the attention to public expenditure management. The room brimmed with anticipation as Director Chanda, an esteemed economist, prepared to unravel the intricacies of expenditure management.

"Public expenditure management is crucial for ensuring that government resources are used efficiently and effectively," Minister Lumamba emphasized, highlighting its significance. "Director Chanda, please enlighten us on the principles guiding expenditure management."

The setting transitioned to a government auditorium, where Director Chanda stood before a group of policymakers and analysts, ready to impart knowledge. Charts and graphs decorated the walls, illustrating budget allocations and expenditure trends.

"Public expenditure management involves the planning, allocation, and monitoring of government spending," Director Chanda explained, capturing the audience's attention. "It aims to maximize the impact of public funds while ensuring accountability and transparency."

The narrative shifted to a community development project site, where workers were engaged in various infrastructure projects. Director Chanda's voiceover elucidated the importance of prioritizing expenditure to address the needs of society.

"Expenditure management requires careful prioritization of

spending to meet the needs and priorities of the population," Director Chanda noted. "Investments in infrastructure, education, healthcare, and social welfare programs play a vital role in promoting inclusive growth and development."

The story then transitioned to a government office, where officials were engaged in budget planning and allocation exercises. Director Chanda's voiceover underscored the importance of transparency and accountability in expenditure management.

"Transparency and accountability are essential principles of expenditure management," Director Chanda emphasized. "Public funds must be used responsibly and in accordance with established rules and regulations to ensure trust and confidence in government institutions."

Back at the Ministry of Finance, the directors absorbed the insights shared by Director Chanda. The room was filled with a sense of enlightenment as they deepened their understanding of expenditure management principles.

Minister Lumamba, acknowledging the importance of responsible spending, said, "Public expenditure management is a critical component of fiscal governance. Let us uphold the principles of transparency, accountability, and efficiency as we allocate resources to meet the needs of our citizens."

The camera panned out, capturing the directors engaged in lively discussions, eager to apply their newfound understanding in shaping Zambia's expenditure policies. The discussion on public expenditure management had provided invaluable insights, empowering them to make informed decisions in the realm of public finance.

2.4 Debt Management Strategies

Minister Mwamba Kabwe sat at his large oak desk, papers spread out before him. His brow was furrowed with concern as he reviewed Zambia's latest economic reports. The numbers were daunting, reflecting a mounting national debt that threatened to undermine the country's economic stability.

"Minister, we need to develop a robust debt management strategy," said Mr. Joseph Lungu, his senior economic advisor, who sat across from him.

Minister Kabwe nodded. "You're right, Joseph. The debt situation is critical, but we must approach it methodically."

The conference room was filled with the Minister's top directors, each bringing their expertise to the table. Among them were Ms. Grace Zulu, Director of Fiscal Policy, and Mr. Robert Nkwazi, Director of Debt Management.

"As you all know," Minister Kabwe began, "our national debt has reached unsustainable levels. Today, we need to outline a comprehensive debt management strategy to ensure fiscal stability and sustainable economic growth."

Ms. Zulu stood up and projected a series of slides onto the screen. "Our first step is to assess the current debt portfolio. We need to understand the composition of our debt—both domestic and external—and identify the most pressing obligations."

Mr. Nkwazi interjected, "We should also consider restructuring our existing debt. Renegotiating terms with our creditors can provide us with some breathing room."

Minister Kabwe nodded. "Agreed. Let's focus on extending maturities and reducing interest rates where possible."

The room buzzed with activity as the directors brainstormed

solutions. Ms. Zulu proposed the issuance of government bonds to raise funds for debt repayment. "This could help us manage our short-term liabilities," she suggested.

Mr. Nkwazi added, "We should also explore debt swaps. Converting high-interest debt into lower-interest or concessional loans can significantly reduce our interest burden."

Minister Kabwe arranged a video conference with representatives from the International Monetary Fund (IMF) and the World Bank. The discussion centered around obtaining technical assistance and advice on best practices for debt management.

"Your technical support will be invaluable in developing a sustainable debt strategy," Minister Kabwe stated. "We need to ensure that our approach aligns with international standards."

Back in Lusaka, the team finalized their debt management strategy. It included measures such as regular debt sustainability analyses, improving transparency in debt reporting, and enhancing the capacity of the Debt Management Office.

"We need to implement strict fiscal discipline," Minister Kabwe emphasized. "Controlling public expenditure and increasing revenue generation will be key to preventing further debt accumulation."

Minister Kabwe stood at a podium, addressing the nation. "Fellow citizens, we are committed to managing our national debt responsibly. Our new strategy aims to stabilize our economy and lay the foundation for sustainable growth. Together, we will overcome this challenge and build a prosperous future for Zambia."

The audience responded with a sense of cautious optimism. The plan was ambitious, but it was also a necessary step toward economic recovery.

Months later, Minister Kabwe and his team reviewed the progress of their debt management strategy. While challenges remained, the initial results were promising. Debt restructuring efforts had borne fruit, and fiscal discipline measures were beginning to take effect.

"There's still a long road ahead," Minister Kabwe remarked, "but we've taken the first critical steps toward securing our nation's economic future."

The team shared a moment of quiet satisfaction, knowing that their efforts were making a tangible difference. Through careful planning and strategic execution, they were navigating Zambia toward a more stable and prosperous economic landscape.

2.5 Financial Institutions and Markets

Continuing the exploration of public finance foundations, Minister Peter Lumamba shifted the focus to financial institutions and markets. The room hummed with anticipation as Director Sibanda, a seasoned economist, prepared to unravel the complexities of financial systems.

"Financial institutions and markets are the backbone of economic activity," Minister Lumamba emphasized, underlining their importance. "Director Sibanda, please shed light on the role of financial institutions and markets in public finance."

The setting transitioned to a financial education seminar, where Director Sibanda stood before a diverse audience, ready to share knowledge. Charts and diagrams adorned the walls, illustrating the intricacies of financial systems.

"Financial institutions play a vital role in facilitating the flow of funds between savers and borrowers," Director Sibanda began, capturing the audience's attention. "Banks, insurance companies, and pension funds are key players in the financial ecosystem, providing essential services to individuals and businesses."

The narrative shifted to a stock exchange trading floor, where traders shouted orders and monitored fluctuating stock prices. Director Sibanda's voiceover elucidated the role of financial markets in mobilizing capital and facilitating investment.

"Financial markets provide a platform for buying and selling financial assets, such as stocks, bonds, and commodities," Director Sibanda noted. "They allocate resources efficiently, allowing investors to diversify their portfolios and manage risk."

The story then transitioned to a meeting with central bank officials, where policymakers discussed monetary policy and interest rate decisions. Director Sibanda's voiceover underscored the role of central banks in regulating financial institutions and maintaining monetary stability.

"Central banks serve as the guardians of financial stability," Director Sibanda emphasized. "They oversee the banking sector, manage the money supply, and set interest rates to achieve price stability and support economic growth."

Back at the Ministry of Finance, the directors absorbed the insights shared by Director Sibanda. The room was filled with a sense of enlightenment as they deepened their understanding of financial systems.

Minister Lumamba, acknowledging the importance of financial institutions and markets, said, "Financial institutions and markets are essential for mobilizing savings, allocating capital, and promoting economic growth. Let us work to strengthen our financial infrastructure and ensure its stability and resilience."

The camera panned out, capturing the directors engaged in lively discussions, eager to apply their newfound understanding in shaping Zambia's financial policies. The discussion on financial institutions and markets had provided invaluable insights, empowering them to make informed decisions in the realm of public finance.

2.6 Economic Development Planning and Policy Formulation

As the exploration of public finance foundations continued, Minister Peter Lumamba directed the attention to economic development planning and policy formulation. The room brimmed with anticipation as Director Patel, an esteemed economist, prepared to unravel the intricacies of economic planning.

"Economic development planning and policy formulation are vital for guiding our nation's growth and prosperity," Minister Lumamba emphasized, highlighting their significance. "Director Patel, please enlighten us on the principles guiding economic planning and policy formulation."

The setting transitioned to a planning workshop within the Ministry of Finance, where Director Patel stood before a group of policymakers and analysts, ready to impart knowledge. Charts and graphs decorated the walls, illustrating economic indicators and development goals.

"Economic development planning involves setting goals and strategies to promote sustainable growth and development," Director Patel began, capturing the audience's attention. "It encompasses policies related to investment, trade, infrastructure, and human capital development."

The narrative shifted to a strategic meeting with sector experts, where policymakers discussed priorities and strategies for economic development. Director Patel's voiceover elucidated the importance of stakeholder engagement and collaboration in policy formulation.

"Policy formulation requires input from a diverse range of stakeholders, including government agencies, private sector actors, civil society organizations, and international partners," Director Patel noted. "Collaborative decision-making ensures that policies are effective, inclusive, and aligned with national development objectives."

The story then transitioned to a field visit to development projects across the country, showcasing investments in infrastructure, agriculture, education, and healthcare. Director Patel's voiceover underscored the role of economic planning in addressing societal needs and fostering inclusive growth.

"Economic planning aims to allocate resources efficiently to meet the needs and aspirations of the population," Director Patel emphasized. "By investing in critical sectors and promoting innovation and entrepreneurship, we can create opportunities for all citizens to participate in and benefit from economic development."

Back at the Ministry of Finance, the directors absorbed the insights shared by Director Patel. The room was filled with a sense of enlightenment as they deepened their understanding of economic planning principles.

Minister Lumamba, acknowledging the importance of economic development planning, said, "Economic planning and policy formulation are essential for guiding our nation towards sustainable development and prosperity. Let us work collaboratively to formulate policies that promote inclusive growth and address the needs of all Zambians."

The camera panned out, capturing the directors engaged in lively discussions, eager to apply their newfound understanding in shaping Zambia's economic policies. The discussion on economic development planning and policy formulation had provided invaluable insights, empowering them to make informed decisions in the realm of public finance.

3

Chapter 3: The Dynamics of International Trade

3.1 Trade Theories and Comparative Advantage

Minister of Commerce, Esther Mukwiza, gathered her team to delve into the dynamics of international trade. The room buzzed with anticipation as Director Mwila, an expert economist, prepared to unravel the theories underpinning trade and comparative advantage.

"Understanding trade theories and comparative advantage is fundamental to our approach to international trade," Minister Mukwiza emphasized, highlighting their importance. "Director Mwila, please enlighten us on the principles guiding trade theories and comparative advantage."

The setting transitioned to a classroom within the Ministry of Commerce, where Director Mwila stood before a group of policymakers and analysts, ready to impart knowledge. Charts and graphs adorned the walls, illustrating economic models and trade flows.

"Trade theories provide frameworks for understanding the patterns and benefits of international trade," Director Mwila began, capturing the audience's attention. "One of the most fundamental theories is the theory of comparative advantage."

The narrative shifted to a rural farming community, where villagers engaged in agricultural activities. Director Mwila's voiceover elucidated the concept of comparative advantage using a simple example.

"Comparative advantage refers to the ability of a country to produce goods or services at a lower opportunity cost than another country," Director Mwila explained. "Even if one country is more efficient at producing all goods, both countries can still benefit from specialization and trade based on their respective comparative advantages."

The story then transitioned to a trade negotiation room, where diplomats engaged in discussions over trade agreements and tariffs. Director Mwila's voiceover underscored the role of comparative advantage in shaping trade policies and negotiations.

"Understanding comparative advantage allows countries to identify their strengths and specialize in the production of goods and services where they have a comparative advantage," Director Mwila noted. "This leads to increased efficiency, higher productivity, and overall welfare gains for all trading partners."

Back at the Ministry of Commerce, the team absorbed the insights shared by Director Mwila. The room was filled with a sense of enlightenment as they deepened their understanding of trade theories and comparative advantage.

Minister Mukwiza, acknowledging the importance of comparative advantage in trade, said, "Trade theories such as comparative advantage guide our approach to international trade, enabling us to maximize the benefits for Zambia. Let us leverage our strengths and engage strategically in the global marketplace."

The camera panned out, capturing the team engaged in lively discussions, eager to apply their newfound understanding in shaping Zambia's trade policies. The exploration of trade theories and comparative advantage had provided invaluable insights, empowering them to navigate the complexities of international trade with confidence.

3.2 Trade Policies and Tariff Structures

Continuing their exploration of international trade dynamics, Minister Esther Mukwiza convened her team to delve into trade policies and tariff structures. The room brimmed with anticipation as Director Banda, a seasoned trade expert, prepared to unravel the intricacies of trade policy formulation.

"Trade policies and tariff structures shape our interactions with the global marketplace," Minister Mukwiza emphasized, underlining their significance. "Director Banda, please enlighten us on the principles guiding trade policies and tariff structures."

The setting transitioned to a policy formulation meeting within the Ministry of Commerce, where Director Banda stood before a group of policymakers and analysts, ready to impart knowledge. Charts and graphs decorated the walls, illustrating trade flows and tariff rates.

"Trade policies encompass a range of measures aimed at regulating and promoting international trade," Director Banda began, capturing the audience's attention. "Tariffs, in particular, are one of the most common trade policy instruments used by governments."

The narrative shifted to a bustling port of entry, where cargo ships unloaded goods from around the world. Director Banda's voiceover elucidated the role of tariffs in influencing trade flows and protecting domestic industries.

"Tariffs are taxes imposed on imported goods, designed to raise revenue for the government and protect domestic industries from foreign competition," Director Banda explained. "They can be used to incentivize domestic production, address trade imbalances, and promote strategic industries."

The story then transitioned to a trade negotiation room, where diplomats engaged in discussions over trade agreements and tariff reductions. Director Banda's voiceover underscored the complexities of trade negotiations and the importance of balancing national interests with international obligations.

"Trade negotiations involve careful consideration of tariff structures and their implications for domestic industries and consumers," Director Banda noted. "Countries seek to negotiate favorable terms that maximize their economic interests while complying with international trade rules and agreements."

Back at the Ministry of Commerce, the team absorbed the insights shared by Director Banda. The room was filled with a sense of enlightenment as they deepened their understanding of trade policies and tariff structures.

Minister Mukwiza, acknowledging the importance of strategic trade policies, said, "Trade policies and tariff structures are powerful tools for promoting economic growth and protecting our industries. Let us formulate policies that strike the right balance between fostering competitiveness and safeguarding our national interests."

The camera panned out, capturing the team engaged in lively discussions, eager to apply their newfound understanding in shaping Zambia's trade policies. The exploration of trade policies and tariff structures had provided invaluable insights, empowering them to navigate the complexities of international trade with confidence.

3.3 Trade Agreements and Regional Integration

As the exploration of international trade dynamics continued, Minister Esther Mukwiza gathered her team to delve into trade agreements and regional integration. The room brimmed with anticipation as Director Kamanga, an expert in trade negotiations, prepared to unravel the complexities of trade agreements.

"Trade agreements and regional integration are key drivers of economic cooperation and growth," Minister Mukwiza emphasized, highlighting their significance. "Director Kamanga, please enlighten us on the principles guiding trade agreements and regional integration."

The setting transitioned to a trade negotiation room within the Ministry of Commerce, where Director Kamanga stood before a group of policymakers and analysts, ready to impart knowledge. Charts and maps adorned the walls, illustrating trade blocs and regional integration initiatives.

"Trade agreements are treaties between countries that govern the terms of trade and investment between them," Director Kamanga began, capturing the audience's attention. "They can range from bilateral agreements between two countries to multilateral agreements involving multiple nations."

The narrative shifted to a map of Africa, highlighting the continent's various regional economic communities. Director Kamanga's voiceover elucidated the importance of regional integration in fostering economic development and cooperation.

"Regional integration aims to promote closer economic ties and cooperation between countries within a specific region," Director Kamanga explained. "It facilitates trade, investment, and the movement of goods and people, leading to shared prosperity and development."

The story then transitioned to a summit of African leaders, where discussions centered on deepening regional integration and strengthening economic cooperation. Director Kamanga's voiceover underscored the significance of regional integration initiatives such as the African Continental Free Trade Area (AfCFTA).

"The AfCFTA represents a landmark agreement aimed at creating a single market for goods and services across the African continent," Director Kamanga noted. "It has the potential to boost intra-African trade, stimulate economic growth, and enhance Africa's global competitiveness."

Back at the Ministry of Commerce, the team absorbed the insights shared by Director Kamanga. The room was filled with a sense of enlightenment as they deepened their understanding of trade agreements and regional integration.

Minister Mukwiza, acknowledging the importance of regional cooperation, said, "Trade agreements and regional integration initiatives are essential for promoting economic development and integration. Let us continue to engage actively in regional initiatives and leverage our partnerships for mutual benefit."

The camera panned out, capturing the team engaged in lively

discussions, eager to apply their newfound understanding in shaping Zambia's trade policies. The exploration of trade agreements and regional integration had provided invaluable insights, empowering them to navigate the complexities of international trade with confidence.

3.4 Foreign Direct Investment (FDI) and Multinational Corporations

Continuing their exploration of international trade dynamics, Minister Esther Mukwiza convened her team to delve into foreign direct investment (FDI) and multinational corporations. The room brimmed with anticipation as Director Lumamba, an expert in investment promotion, prepared to unravel the intricacies of FDI and multinational operations.

"Foreign direct investment and multinational corporations play a significant role in shaping global trade and economic development," Minister Mukwiza emphasized, highlighting their importance. "Director Lumamba, please enlighten us on the principles guiding FDI and multinational corporations."

The setting transitioned to a seminar on investment promotion within the Ministry of Commerce, where Director Lumamba stood before a group of policymakers and analysts, ready to impart knowledge. Graphs and charts adorned the walls, illustrating investment trends and multinational operations.

"Foreign direct investment refers to the investment made by a company or individual from one country into another," Director Lumamba began, capturing the audience's attention. "It can take various forms, including the establishment of new businesses, acquisitions, or joint ventures."

The narrative shifted to a global business forum, where executives from multinational corporations discussed investment opportunities and market trends. Director Lumamba's voiceover elucidated the role of multinational corporations in driving global trade and investment flows.

"Multinational corporations operate across borders, leveraging their resources and expertise to expand into new markets and drive economic growth," Director Lumamba explained. "They bring capital, technology, and managerial know-how, stimulating innovation and creating employment opportunities."

The story then transitioned to a foreign investment expo, where Zambian officials showcased investment opportunities to potential foreign investors. Director Lumamba's voiceover underscored the importance of attracting FDI to foster economic development and industrialization.

"Attracting foreign direct investment is crucial for Zambia's economic development," Director Lumamba noted. "It provides access to capital, technology, and markets, driving productivity gains and fostering industrialization and diversification."

Back at the Ministry of Commerce, the team absorbed the insights shared by Director Lumamba. The room was filled with a sense of enlightenment as they deepened their understanding of FDI and multinational operations.

Minister Mukwiza, acknowledging the importance of attracting investment, said, "Foreign direct investment and multinational corporations are essential drivers of economic growth and development. Let us continue to create an enabling environment for investment and leverage our partnerships to attract sustainable FDI."

The camera panned out, capturing the team engaged in lively discussions, eager to apply their newfound understanding in shaping Zambia's investment promotion strategies. The exploration of FDI and multinational corporations had provided invaluable insights, empowering them to navigate the complexities of international trade with confidence.

3.5 Exchange Rates and Currency Markets

Continuing their exploration of international trade dynamics, Minister Esther Mukwiza convened her team to delve into exchange rates and currency markets. The room brimmed with anticipation as Director Chilufya, an expert economist, prepared to unravel the intricacies of exchange rate mechanisms.

"Exchange rates and currency markets play a pivotal role in facilitating international trade and investment," Minister Mukwiza emphasized, highlighting their significance. "Director Chilufya, please enlighten us on the principles guiding exchange rates and currency markets."

The setting transitioned to a currency trading room within the Ministry of Commerce, where Director Chilufya stood before a group of policymakers and analysts, ready to impart knowledge. Screens displayed real-time exchange rates and currency fluctuations.

"Exchange rates represent the value of one currency relative to another," Director Chilufya began, capturing the audience's attention. "They determine the cost of goods and services in international markets and influence trade flows and investment decisions."

The narrative shifted to a global economic summit, where

policymakers and central bank officials discussed exchange rate policies and currency stability. Director Chilufya's voiceover elucidated the factors influencing exchange rate movements and their implications for trade.

"Exchange rates are influenced by a myriad of factors, including interest rates, inflation, economic growth, and geopolitical events," Director Chilufya explained. "Changes in exchange rates can affect the competitiveness of exports and imports, as well as the profitability of international investments."

The story then transitioned to a meeting of central bank officials, where policymakers discussed monetary policy and exchange rate interventions. Director Chilufya's voiceover underscored the role of central banks in maintaining currency stability and managing exchange rate fluctuations.

"Central banks play a crucial role in influencing exchange rates through monetary policy tools such as interest rate adjustments and foreign exchange market interventions," Director Chilufya noted. "They aim to maintain price stability and support economic growth while ensuring exchange rate competitiveness."

Back at the Ministry of Commerce, the team absorbed the insights shared by Director Chilufya. The room was filled with a sense of enlightenment as they deepened their understanding of exchange rates and currency markets.

Minister Mukwiza, acknowledging the importance of exchange rate stability, said, "Exchange rates and currency markets are essential determinants of international trade and investment. Let us work to ensure exchange rate stability and promote a conducive environment for trade and investment."

The camera panned out, capturing the team engaged in lively discussions, eager to apply their newfound understanding in shaping Zambia's exchange rate policies. The exploration of exchange rates and currency markets had provided invaluable insights, empowering them to navigate the complexities of international trade with confidence.

3.6 Trade Facilitation and Supply Chain Management

Continuing their exploration of international trade dynamics, Minister Esther Mukwiza convened her team to delve into trade facilitation and supply chain management. The room brimmed with anticipation as Director Sibanda, an expert in logistics and trade facilitation, prepared to unravel the intricacies of supply chain management.

"Trade facilitation and supply chain management are critical components of international trade," Minister Mukwiza emphasized, highlighting their significance. "Director Sibanda, please enlighten us on the principles guiding trade facilitation and supply chain management."

The setting transitioned to a logistics planning room within the Ministry of Commerce, where Director Sibanda stood before a group of policymakers and analysts, ready to impart knowledge. Maps and charts adorned the walls, illustrating trade routes and logistics networks.

"Supply chain management involves the coordination of activities to ensure the seamless flow of goods and services from production to consumption," Director Sibanda began, capturing the audience's attention. "Efficient supply chains reduce costs, minimize delays, and enhance competitiveness."

The narrative shifted to a customs clearance facility, where officials processed imports and exports efficiently. Director Sibanda's voiceover elucidated the role of trade facilitation measures in streamlining border procedures and reducing trade barriers.

"Trade facilitation measures such as simplified customs procedures, electronic documentation, and single window systems expedite the movement of goods across borders," Director Sibanda explained. "They reduce transaction costs and enhance the efficiency of international trade."

The story then transitioned to a warehouse management center, where workers organized and managed inventory with precision. Director Sibanda's voiceover underscored the importance of efficient logistics and inventory management in optimizing supply chain performance.

"Effective warehouse management ensures that goods are stored, handled, and distributed efficiently," Director Sibanda noted. "It reduces inventory holding costs, minimizes stock-outs, and improves customer satisfaction."

Back at the Ministry of Commerce, the team absorbed the insights shared by Director Sibanda. The room was filled with a sense of enlightenment as they deepened their understanding of trade facilitation and supply chain management.

Minister Mukwiza, acknowledging the importance of efficient supply chains, said, "Trade facilitation and supply chain management are essential for reducing trade costs and enhancing competitiveness. Let us continue to invest in infrastructure and streamline procedures to facilitate trade and promote economic growth."

The camera panned out, capturing the team engaged in lively discussions, eager to apply their newfound understanding in shaping Zambia's trade facilitation strategies. The exploration of trade facilitation and supply chain management had provided invaluable insights, empowering them to navigate the complexities of international trade with confidence.

4

Chapter 4: Macroeconomic Policy Coordination

4.1 Monetary Policy and Central Banking

As the exploration of macroeconomic policy coordination began, Governor Peter Lumamba gathered his team at the Central Bank of Zambia to delve into monetary policy and central banking. The room buzzed with anticipation as Director Mulenga, a seasoned economist, prepared to elucidate the intricacies of monetary policy.

"Monetary policy and central banking are critical pillars of macroeconomic stability," Governor Lumamba emphasized, underlining their significance. "Director Mulenga, please enlighten us on the principles guiding monetary policy and central banking."

The setting transitioned to the central bank's boardroom, where Director Mulenga stood before a group of policymakers and analysts, ready to impart knowledge. Charts and graphs adorned the walls, illustrating economic indicators and mone-

CHAPTER 4: MACROECONOMIC POLICY COORDINATION

tary policy tools.

"Monetary policy refers to the actions taken by the central bank to control the money supply and achieve macroeconomic objectives," Director Mulenga began, capturing the audience's attention. "It aims to maintain price stability, support economic growth, and ensure financial stability."

The narrative shifted to a meeting of the monetary policy committee, where policymakers discussed interest rate decisions and inflation forecasts. Director Mulenga's voiceover elucidated the role of monetary policy in influencing economic variables such as inflation and employment.

"The central bank uses various monetary policy tools, including interest rates, reserve requirements, and open market operations, to achieve its objectives," Director Mulenga explained. "By adjusting these tools, the central bank can influence borrowing and spending behavior, thereby affecting economic outcomes."

The story then transitioned to a banking regulation seminar, where central bank officials discussed regulatory frameworks and financial stability measures. Director Mulenga's voiceover underscored the importance of central bank oversight in safeguarding the stability of the financial system.

"Central banks play a crucial role in regulating banks and financial institutions to ensure the safety and soundness of the banking system," Director Mulenga noted. "They establish prudential regulations, conduct supervisory assessments, and provide liquidity support to maintain financial stability."

Back at the central bank, the team absorbed the insights shared by Director Mulenga. The room was filled with a sense of enlightenment as they deepened their understanding of monetary policy and central banking.

Governor Lumamba, acknowledging the importance of central bank independence, said, "Monetary policy and central banking are essential for maintaining macroeconomic stability and financial resilience. Let us continue to uphold the principles of central bank independence and transparency in our policymaking."

The camera panned out, capturing the team engaged in lively discussions, eager to apply their newfound understanding in shaping Zambia's monetary policy framework. The exploration of monetary policy and central banking had provided invaluable insights, empowering them to navigate the complexities of macroeconomic policy coordination with confidence.

4.2 Exchange Rate Regimes and Policy Options

Continuing their exploration of macroeconomic policy coordination, Minister of Finance Peter Lumamba convened his team to delve into exchange rate regimes and policy options. The room hummed with anticipation as Director Chanda, an esteemed economist, prepared to unravel the intricacies of exchange rate policies.

"Exchange rate regimes and policy options are crucial elements of macroeconomic management," Minister Lumamba emphasized, highlighting their significance. "Director Chanda, please enlighten us on the principles guiding exchange rate regimes and policy options."

The setting transitioned to the ministry's conference room, where Director Chanda stood before a group of policymakers and analysts, ready to impart knowledge. Charts and graphs decorated the walls, illustrating exchange rate trends and policy alternatives.

"Exchange rate regimes determine how a country manages its currency in relation to others," Director Chanda began, capturing the audience's attention. "They range from fixed regimes, where the exchange rate is pegged to another currency or a basket of currencies, to floating regimes, where the exchange rate is determined by market forces."

The narrative shifted to a simulation of exchange rate fluctuations, where economists analyzed the effects of different exchange rate regimes on the economy. Director Chanda's voiceover elucidated the trade-offs associated with each regime and the policy options available to policymakers.

"Fixed exchange rate regimes offer stability and predictability but may require intervention by the central bank to maintain the peg," Director Chanda explained. "Floating exchange rate regimes allow for greater flexibility and automatic adjustment to market conditions but may lead to volatility and uncertainty."

The story then transitioned to a policy debate in parliament, where lawmakers discussed the merits of different exchange rate regimes and policy options. Director Chanda's voiceover underscored the importance of aligning exchange rate policies with broader macroeconomic objectives.

"The choice of exchange rate regime depends on various factors, including the country's economic structure, external vulnerabilities, and policy preferences," Director Chanda noted. "Policymakers must weigh the benefits and costs of each regime and adopt measures to mitigate potential risks."

Back at the Ministry of Finance, the team absorbed the insights shared by Director Chanda. The room was filled with a sense of enlightenment as they deepened their understanding of exchange rate regimes and policy options.

Minister Lumamba, acknowledging the complexity of exchange rate policies, said, "Exchange rate regimes and policy options require careful consideration and strategic planning. Let us work collaboratively to formulate policies that promote stability, competitiveness, and sustainable economic growth."

The camera panned out, capturing the team engaged in lively discussions, eager to apply their newfound understanding in shaping Zambia's exchange rate policies. The exploration of exchange rate regimes and policy options had provided invaluable insights, empowering them to navigate the complexities of macroeconomic policy coordination with confidence.

4.3 Inflation Targeting and Price Stability

As the exploration of macroeconomic policy coordination continued, Governor Peter Lumamba gathered his team at the Central Bank of Zambia to delve into inflation targeting and price stability. The room buzzed with anticipation as Director Ngoma, an esteemed economist, prepared to elucidate the intricacies of inflation targeting.

"Inflation targeting and price stability are cornerstones of macroeconomic policy," Governor Lumamba emphasized, underlining their significance. "Director Ngoma, please enlighten us on the principles guiding inflation targeting and price stability."

The setting transitioned to the central bank's boardroom, where Director Ngoma stood before a group of policymakers and analysts, ready to impart knowledge. Charts and graphs adorned the walls, illustrating inflation trends and monetary policy frameworks.

"Inflation targeting is a monetary policy framework aimed at achieving a specific inflation rate within a defined target range," Director Ngoma began, capturing the audience's attention. "It involves setting clear inflation targets and using interest rate adjustments to achieve them."

The narrative shifted to an economic forum, where experts discussed the benefits of inflation targeting in promoting price stability and anchoring inflation expectations. Director Ngoma's voiceover elucidated the importance of maintaining price stability for sustainable economic growth.

"Price stability is essential for preserving the purchasing power of money and fostering confidence in the economy," Director Ngoma explained. "By targeting low and stable inflation, central banks can create a conducive environment for investment, consumption, and long-term planning."

The story then transitioned to a policy announcement by the central bank, where Governor Lumamba unveiled the latest inflation target and monetary policy stance. Director Ngoma's voiceover underscored the central bank's commitment to achieving price stability and anchoring inflation expectations.

"Inflation targeting provides a transparent and credible framework for monetary policy decision-making," Director Ngoma noted. "By communicating clear objectives and policy actions, central banks can enhance the effectiveness of monetary policy and guide economic agents' behavior."

Back at the central bank, the team absorbed the insights shared by Director Ngoma. The room was filled with a sense of enlightenment as they deepened their understanding of inflation targeting and price stability.

Governor Lumamba, acknowledging the importance of maintaining price stability, said, "Inflation targeting is a powerful tool for anchoring inflation expectations and promoting economic stability. Let us continue to pursue sound monetary policies that support sustainable growth and prosperity."

The camera panned out, capturing the team engaged in lively discussions, eager to apply their newfound understanding in shaping Zambia's monetary policy framework. The exploration of inflation targeting and price stability had provided invaluable insights, empowering them to navigate the complexities of macroeconomic policy coordination with confidence.

4.4 Coordination of Fiscal and Monetary Policies

Continuing their exploration of macroeconomic policy coordination, Minister of Finance Peter Lumamba and Governor Peter Lumamba convened a joint meeting at the Ministry of Finance and the Central Bank of Zambia to discuss the coordination of fiscal and monetary policies. The room hummed with anticipation as policymakers and economists prepared to address the complexities of policy coordination.

"Fiscal and monetary policies must work hand in hand to achieve macroeconomic stability and sustainable growth," Minister Lumamba emphasized, highlighting the importance of coordination. "Let us explore the principles guiding the coordination of fiscal and monetary policies."

The setting transitioned to a meeting table, where Minister Lumamba and Governor Lumamba sat at the head, flanked by policymakers and economists from both institutions. Charts and reports scattered across the table, illustrating economic indicators and policy options.

"Fiscal policy refers to the government's use of taxation and spending to influence economic activity," Minister Lumamba began, addressing the audience. "Monetary policy, on the other hand, involves the central bank's control over the money supply and interest rates to achieve macroeconomic objectives."

The narrative shifted to a policy discussion, where policymakers debated the appropriate stance for fiscal and monetary policies given the current economic conditions. Views varied, with some advocating for expansionary measures to stimulate growth, while others emphasized the need for prudence to maintain stability.

"Coordination of fiscal and monetary policies is essential to avoid conflicting objectives and achieve macroeconomic balance," Governor Lumamba noted, emphasizing the importance of policy alignment. "Effective communication and collaboration between the Ministry of Finance and the central bank are paramount."

The story then transitioned to a joint policy announcement, where Minister Lumamba and Governor Lumamba unveiled a coordinated approach to fiscal and monetary policies. Their joint statement outlined measures to support economic recovery while safeguarding price stability and fiscal sustainability.

"By coordinating fiscal and monetary policies, we aim to achieve our dual mandate of promoting economic growth and maintaining price stability," Minister Lumamba announced, echoing Governor Lumamba's sentiments. "Together, we will ensure that our policies support sustainable and inclusive development for all Zambians."

Back in the joint meeting room, policymakers and economists absorbed the outcomes of the discussion. The room was filled with a sense of unity and purpose as they recognized the importance of coordinated policy action in navigating the challenges ahead.

Governor Lumamba and Minister Lumamba exchanged

nods of approval, signaling their commitment to continued collaboration in steering Zambia towards prosperity. The joint coordination of fiscal and monetary policies had provided a framework for cohesive action, empowering them to address economic challenges with confidence and determination.

4.5 Global Economic Governance and Institutions

Continuing their exploration of macroeconomic policy coordination, Minister of Finance Peter Lumamba and Governor Peter Lumamba joined leaders from around the world at an International Economic Summit in Geneva, Switzerland, to discuss global economic governance and institutions. The grand hall buzzed with anticipation as policymakers and experts from various countries gathered to address the challenges of global economic coordination.

"Global economic governance and institutions play a crucial role in shaping the international economic landscape," Minister Lumamba emphasized, addressing the audience. "Let us explore the principles guiding global economic governance and the role of international institutions in promoting stability and cooperation."

The setting transitioned to the summit stage, where Minister Lumamba and Governor Lumamba stood before a diverse audience of world leaders and dignitaries. Behind them, a backdrop displayed the logos of international organizations and institutions.

"Global economic governance refers to the framework of rules, agreements, and institutions that govern international economic relations," Governor Lumamba explained, capturing the attention of the audience. "It encompasses a range of issues,

CHAPTER 4: MACROECONOMIC POLICY COORDINATION

including trade, finance, development, and sustainability."

The narrative shifted to a panel discussion, where experts from international institutions and academia exchanged views on the challenges and opportunities of global economic governance. Views varied, with some highlighting the need for reform to address emerging threats, while others emphasized the importance of multilateral cooperation in tackling global issues.

"The effectiveness of global economic governance depends on the strength and inclusivity of international institutions," remarked Minister Lumamba, echoing the sentiments of the panelists. "We must work together to ensure that these institutions are equipped to address the complex challenges of the 21st century."

The story then transitioned to a bilateral meeting between Minister Lumamba and a counterpart from another country, where they discussed opportunities for collaboration and cooperation on global economic issues. Their dialogue underscored the importance of building alliances and fostering mutual understanding to advance common goals.

"As representatives of our respective countries, it is incumbent upon us to champion the principles of transparency, accountability, and fairness in global economic governance," Minister Lumamba affirmed, emphasizing the need for principled leadership on the world stage.

Back at the International Economic Summit, policymakers and experts absorbed the outcomes of the discussions and deliberations. The hall echoed with the buzz of conversation as participants exchanged insights and ideas, united in their commitment to strengthening global economic governance and institutions.

Minister Lumamba and Governor Lumamba exchanged nods of agreement, acknowledging the progress made and the challenges that lay ahead. The summit had provided a platform for constructive dialogue and collaboration, paving the way for enhanced cooperation in addressing the complex economic issues facing the world today.

4.5 Global Economic Governance and Institutions

Continuing their exploration of macroeconomic policy coordination, Minister of Finance Peter Lumamba and Governor Peter Lumamba found themselves at the United Nations Headquarters in New York City, among leaders from around the globe. They were there to participate in a high-level summit on global economic governance and institutions. The room hummed with anticipation as representatives from various nations gathered to address the challenges and opportunities of international economic cooperation.

"Global economic governance and institutions are the cornerstone of a stable and prosperous world economy," Minister Lumamba emphasized, his voice echoing in the grand assembly hall. "Let us explore how we can strengthen these institutions to foster cooperation and address global economic challenges."

The setting transitioned to the summit stage, where Minister Lumamba and Governor Lumamba stood at the podium, facing a diverse audience of world leaders and delegates. Behind them, the flags of member states fluttered in the gentle breeze, symbolizing unity and collaboration.

"Global economic governance encompasses a wide range of issues, including trade, finance, development, and environmental sustainability," Governor Lumamba began, his voice commanding the attention of the audience. "It requires strong institutions and effective cooperation among nations to address the complex interdependencies of the global economy."

The narrative shifted to a roundtable discussion, where leaders engaged in a spirited exchange of ideas and perspectives on global economic governance. Views varied, with some advocating for greater inclusivity and representation in international institutions, while others emphasized the importance of collective action to address global challenges.

"As leaders, we have a responsibility to ensure that global economic governance is transparent, accountable, and responsive to the needs of all nations," Minister Lumamba asserted, echoing the sentiments of the participants. "By working together, we can build a more resilient and equitable global economy."

The story then transitioned to a bilateral meeting between Minister Lumamba and a counterpart from another country, where they discussed opportunities for collaboration and partnership on global economic issues. Their dialogue underscored the importance of building trust and understanding to overcome shared challenges.

"As representatives of our respective nations, we must uphold the principles of fairness and cooperation in all our interactions," Minister Lumamba affirmed, reaffirming his commitment to international cooperation.

Back at the United Nations Headquarters, participants reflected on the discussions and deliberations of the summit. The room buzzed with energy and optimism as leaders exchanged ideas and forged new partnerships to advance the cause of global economic governance and institutions.

Minister Lumamba and Governor Lumamba shared a moment of quiet satisfaction, knowing that their contributions had helped to shape the future of international economic cooperation. The summit had been a testament to the power of dialogue and collaboration in addressing the complex challenges of the modern world.

4.6 Crisis Management and Economic Resilience Strategies

In the heart of Lusaka, Minister of Finance Peter Lumamba and Governor Peter Lumamba convened at the Crisis Management Center to address crisis management and economic resilience strategies. The atmosphere was tense, yet focused, as policymakers and experts gathered to tackle the challenges of economic crises.

"Crisis management and economic resilience are vital in safeguarding our nation's prosperity," Minister Lumamba declared, his voice resolute. "Let us explore strategies to mitigate the impact of crises and build a more resilient economy."

The setting transitioned to the crisis management room, where Minister Lumamba and Governor Lumamba led a team of advisors in analyzing economic data and formulating strategies. Screens flickered with real-time updates on market indicators and crisis scenarios.

"Economic crises can take many forms, from financial market disruptions to natural disasters," Governor Lumamba explained, his tone urgent. "It is essential to have robust crisis management protocols in place to respond swiftly and effectively."

The narrative shifted to a crisis simulation exercise, where policymakers role-played different crisis scenarios and tested their response strategies. Tensions ran high as they grappled with difficult decisions and sought to minimize the impact on the economy.

"As leaders, we must remain calm and decisive in the face of crisis," Minister Lumamba asserted, rallying his team. "By working together and leveraging our strengths, we can overcome any challenge that comes our way."

The story then transitioned to an economic resilience workshop, where experts shared best practices and innovative strategies for building a more resilient economy. Discussions ranged from diversifying revenue streams to investing in infrastructure and human capital.

"Economic resilience requires a multi-faceted approach, encompassing fiscal, monetary, and structural reforms," Governor Lumamba emphasized, his voice echoing the sentiments of the participants. "By building resilience into our economic policies, we can better withstand shocks and emerge stronger than before."

Back at the Crisis Management Center, Minister Lumamba and Governor Lumamba reflected on the outcomes of their discussions and workshops. The room buzzed with a sense of purpose as they reaffirmed their commitment to strengthening crisis management and economic resilience.

"In times of crisis, leadership and cooperation are paramount," Minister Lumamba declared, his gaze unwavering. "Let us continue to work together to build a more resilient and prosperous future for all Zambians."

The camera panned out, capturing the determination and resolve of the team as they prepared to face whatever challenges lay ahead. The exploration of crisis management and economic resilience had provided invaluable insights, empowering them to navigate the complexities of macroeconomic policy coordination with confidence and resilience.

5

Chapter 5: Trade and Development

5.1 Trade and Sustainable Development Goals (SDGs)

Minister of Trade and Development Esther Mukwiza, accompanied by her team, stepped into the bustling halls of the United Nations Conference on Trade and Development (UNCTAD) in Geneva. The air was alive with anticipation as representatives from across the globe gathered to discuss the intersection of trade and the Sustainable Development Goals (SDGs).

"Trade has the power to drive progress towards achieving the Sustainable Development Goals," Minister Mukwiza declared, her voice echoing through the halls. "Let us explore how we can harness the potential of trade to promote sustainable development."

The setting transitioned to the UNCTAD plenary session, where Minister Mukwiza stood before a diverse audience of policymakers, economists, and civil society representatives. Behind her, the flags of member states waved in solidarity, symbolizing the shared commitment to sustainable development.

"Trade plays a pivotal role in advancing the Sustainable Development Goals, from poverty alleviation to gender equality and environmental sustainability," Minister Mukwiza began, capturing the attention of the audience. "By promoting inclusive and sustainable trade policies, we can create opportunities for all and leave no one behind."

The narrative shifted to a panel discussion, where experts delved into the various ways in which trade can contribute to achieving the SDGs. Discussions ranged from enhancing market access for developing countries to promoting sustainable production and consumption patterns.

"Trade can serve as a powerful engine for economic growth and poverty reduction, but it must be inclusive and sustainable," remarked one panelist, echoing the sentiments of the group. "By integrating environmental and social considerations into trade policies, we can ensure that trade contributes to sustainable development."

Scene Transition A Workshop on Trade Capacity Building

The story then transitioned to a workshop on trade capacity building, where participants exchanged best practices and innovative strategies for building trade-related skills and institutions in developing countries. Discussions focused on enhancing trade facilitation, promoting SMEs, and harnessing digital technologies for trade.

"Trade capacity building is essential for empowering developing countries to participate effectively in the global economy," Minister Mukwiza affirmed, her voice filled with conviction.

"By investing in skills development and institutional strengthening, we can unlock the full potential of trade for sustainable development."

Back at the UNCTAD conference, participants reflected on the discussions and insights shared throughout the event. The halls buzzed with excitement as they exchanged ideas and forged new partnerships to advance the cause of trade and sustainable development.

Minister Mukwiza and her team shared a moment of satisfaction, knowing that their contributions had helped to shape the global dialogue on trade and development. The conference had been a testament to the transformative power of trade in driving progress towards the Sustainable Development Goals, and they were inspired to continue their efforts in promoting inclusive and sustainable trade for the benefit of all.

5.2 Trade-Related Aspects of Intellectual Property Rights

Minister of Trade and Development Esther Mukwiza, accompanied by her delegation, entered the grand halls of the World Trade Organization (WTO) headquarters in Geneva. The atmosphere was charged with anticipation as representatives from member states gathered to discuss the trade-related aspects of intellectual property rights (TRIPS).

"Intellectual property rights play a crucial role in fostering innovation and promoting economic development," Minister Mukwiza declared, her voice resonating in the majestic surroundings of the WTO headquarters. "Let us explore how we can strike a balance between protecting intellectual property and promoting access to essential goods and technologies."

The setting transitioned to the WTO plenary session, where

Minister Mukwiza stood before a diverse audience of trade ministers, diplomats, and intellectual property experts. The flags of member states stood proudly in the background, symbolizing the unity of purpose in addressing trade-related intellectual property issues.

"Trade-related aspects of intellectual property rights have a significant impact on access to essential medicines, technology transfer, and cultural diversity," Minister Mukwiza began, capturing the attention of the audience. "It is imperative that we find solutions that promote innovation while ensuring access to vital goods and technologies for all."

The narrative shifted to a roundtable discussion, where experts debated the importance of TRIPS flexibilities in balancing the interests of intellectual property rights holders and public health concerns. Discussions centered on issues such as compulsory licensing, parallel imports, and technology transfer.

"TRIPS flexibilities provide vital policy space for governments to address public health emergencies and promote access to affordable medicines," remarked one participant, reflecting the sentiments of the group. "By leveraging these flexibilities, we can ensure that intellectual property rights serve the public interest."

The story then transitioned to a workshop on technology transfer and capacity building, where participants shared best practices and innovative strategies for promoting technology transfer and building local innovation capabilities in developing countries. Discussions focused on enhancing access to technology, strengthening intellectual property management, and fostering collaboration between public and private sectors.

"Technology transfer is essential for unlocking the potential of innovation and driving economic development," Minister Mukwiza affirmed, her voice filled with determination. "By fostering a conducive environment for technology transfer and capacity building, we can empower developing countries to harness the benefits of intellectual property rights for sustainable development."

Back at the WTO headquarters, participants reflected on the discussions and insights shared throughout the event. The halls buzzed with excitement as they exchanged ideas and forged new partnerships to advance the cause of trade and intellectual property rights.

Minister Mukwiza and her delegation shared a moment of satisfaction, knowing that their contributions had helped to shape the global dialogue on trade-related aspects of intellectual property rights. The discussions had been a testament to the importance of striking a balance between innovation and access, and they were inspired to continue their efforts in promoting inclusive and sustainable trade for the benefit of all.

5.3 Trade and Environmental Sustainability

Minister of Trade and Development Esther Mukwiza, accompanied by her delegation, arrived at the International Environmental Summit in Paris. The venue hummed with anticipation as representatives from nations worldwide gathered to discuss the critical intersection of trade and environmental sustainability.

"Trade has the power to drive both economic growth and environmental degradation," Minister Mukwiza declared, her voice carrying through the conference hall. "Let us explore how we can harness the potential of trade to promote environmental sustainability and combat climate change."

The setting transitioned to the summit stage, where Minister Mukwiza stood before a diverse audience of environmentalists, policymakers, and trade experts. A large screen behind her displayed images of lush forests, pristine oceans, and renewable energy sources.

"Trade and environmental sustainability are not mutually exclusive," Minister Mukwiza began, commanding the attention of the audience. "By adopting trade policies that prioritize environmental protection and conservation, we can create a more sustainable future for generations to come."

The narrative shifted to a panel discussion, where experts explored the potential of sustainable trade practices in promoting environmental conservation and combating climate change. Discussions ranged from green supply chains to renewable energy trade and sustainable agriculture.

"Sustainable trade practices offer opportunities for economic growth while minimizing environmental impact," remarked one panelist, echoing the sentiments of the group. "By integrating environmental considerations into trade policies, we can achieve both economic prosperity and environmental sustainability."

The story then transitioned to a workshop on green trade agreements, where participants exchanged best practices and innovative strategies for incorporating environmental provisions into trade agreements. Discussions focused on issues such as carbon pricing, environmental labeling, and sustainable procurement.

"Green trade agreements can incentivize sustainable production and consumption patterns," Minister Mukwiza affirmed, her voice resonating with conviction. "By promoting trade that respects environmental standards and safeguards, we can create a more sustainable global economy."

Back at the International Environmental Summit, participants reflected on the discussions and insights shared throughout the event. The venue buzzed with energy as they exchanged ideas and forged new partnerships to advance the cause of trade and environmental sustainability.

Minister Mukwiza and her delegation shared a moment of satisfaction, knowing that their contributions had helped to shape the global dialogue on sustainable trade practices. The summit had been a testament to the transformative power of trade in promoting environmental conservation and combating climate change, and they were inspired to continue their efforts in building a more sustainable future for all.

5.4 Trade, Gender, and Social Inclusion

Minister of Trade and Development Esther Mukwiza, accompanied by her delegation, arrived at the International Gender Equality Forum in New York City. The venue buzzed with excitement as delegates from around the world gathered to discuss the intersection of trade, gender, and social inclusion.

"Trade has the potential to empower women and promote social inclusion, but it also poses challenges," Minister Mukwiza declared, her voice resonating with determination. "Let us explore how we can ensure that trade policies benefit all members of society, regardless of gender or background."

The setting transitioned to the forum stage, where Minister Mukwiza stood before a diverse audience of gender equality advocates, policymakers, and trade experts. A large screen behind her displayed images of women entrepreneurs, artisans, and workers from different corners of the globe.

"Women play a vital role in trade and economic development, yet they often face barriers and inequalities," Minister Mukwiza began, capturing the attention of the audience. "By adopting trade policies that promote gender equality and social inclusion, we can unlock the full potential of all members of society."

The narrative shifted to a panel discussion, where experts explored the challenges and opportunities faced by women in trade. Discussions ranged from access to finance and market opportunities to gender-responsive trade policies and capacity-building initiatives.

"Women entrepreneurs and workers are engines of economic growth and innovation," remarked one panelist, echoing the sentiments of the group. "By addressing gender disparities and promoting women's participation in trade, we can create more inclusive and equitable societies."

The story then transitioned to a workshop on gender-responsive trade policies, where participants shared best practices and innovative strategies for mainstreaming gender considerations into trade agreements and programs. Discussions focused on issues such as women's access to trade finance, market access, and capacity building.

"Gender-responsive trade policies are essential for ensuring that trade benefits women and promotes their economic empowerment," Minister Mukwiza affirmed, her voice filled with conviction. "By prioritizing gender equality and social inclusion, we can build a more just and prosperous world for all."

Back at the International Gender Equality Forum, participants reflected on the discussions and insights shared throughout the event. The venue buzzed with energy as they exchanged ideas and forged new partnerships to advance the cause of gender equality and social inclusion.

Minister Mukwiza and her delegation shared a moment of satisfaction, knowing that their contributions had helped to shape the global dialogue on trade, gender, and social inclusion. The forum had been a testament to the transformative power of trade in promoting gender equality and empowering women, and they were inspired to continue their efforts in building a more inclusive and equitable world for all.

5.5 Trade and Poverty Alleviation Strategies

Minister of Trade and Development Esther Mukwiza, accompanied by her delegation, entered the United Nations Headquarters in New York City. The atmosphere was charged with anticipation as representatives from across the globe gathered to discuss the role of trade in poverty alleviation strategies.

"Trade has the potential to lift millions out of poverty, but it must be inclusive and equitable," Minister Mukwiza declared, her voice echoing through the grand halls of the UN Headquarters. "Let us explore how we can harness the power of trade to create opportunities for the world's poorest communities."

The setting transitioned to the summit stage, where Minister Mukwiza stood before a diverse audience of world leaders, economists, and development practitioners. The flags of member states stood tall, symbolizing the collective commitment to eradicating poverty through trade.

"Trade can serve as a powerful engine for economic growth and poverty reduction, but it must be accompanied by targeted policies and interventions," Minister Mukwiza began, capturing the attention of the audience. "By prioritizing the needs of the most vulnerable, we can ensure that trade benefits everyone, regardless of their socio-economic status."

The narrative shifted to a panel discussion, where experts explored the linkages between trade and poverty alleviation. Discussions ranged from access to markets and value chains to trade capacity building and investment in human capital.

"Trade has the potential to create jobs, increase incomes, and improve livelihoods in impoverished communities," remarked one panelist, reflecting the sentiments of the group. "By fostering an enabling environment for trade and investment, we can unlock opportunities for poverty reduction and sustainable development."

The story then transitioned to a workshop on trade capacity building, where participants shared best practices and innovative strategies for building trade-related skills and institutions in developing countries. Discussions focused on issues such as market access, export diversification, and trade facilitation.

"Trade capacity building is essential for empowering developing countries to harness the benefits of trade for poverty alleviation," Minister Mukwiza affirmed, her voice filled with conviction. "By investing in skills development and institutional strengthening, we can create pathways out of poverty for millions of people around the world."

Back at the UN Headquarters, participants reflected on the discussions and insights shared throughout the event. The halls buzzed with energy as they exchanged ideas and forged new partnerships to advance the cause of trade and poverty alleviation.

Minister Mukwiza and her delegation shared a moment of

satisfaction, knowing that their contributions had helped to shape the global dialogue on trade and poverty alleviation strategies. The summit had been a testament to the transformative power of trade in lifting people out of poverty, and they were inspired to continue their efforts in building a more inclusive and prosperous world for all.

5.6 Trade and Human Rights Considerations

Minister of Trade and Development Esther Mukwiza, accompanied by her delegation, entered the Human Rights Council at the United Nations Headquarters in Geneva. The atmosphere was solemn as representatives from nations worldwide gathered to discuss the intersection of trade and human rights considerations.

"Trade policies must uphold human rights principles and respect the dignity and rights of all individuals," Minister Mukwiza declared, her voice firm and unwavering. "Let us explore how we can ensure that trade contributes to the promotion and protection of human rights."

The setting transitioned to the assembly hall, where Minister Mukwiza stood before a diverse audience of human rights advocates, diplomats, and trade experts. The flags of member states stood tall, symbolizing the collective commitment to advancing human rights through trade.

"Trade can have both positive and negative impacts on human rights, depending on how it is conducted and regulated," Minister Mukwiza began, capturing the attention of the audience. "By integrating human rights considerations into trade policies, we can mitigate risks and maximize benefits for all."

The narrative shifted to a panel discussion, where experts delved into the complexities of balancing trade interests with human rights considerations. Discussions ranged from labor rights and environmental protection to indigenous rights and access to essential services.

"Trade agreements should include provisions that safeguard human rights and ensure accountability for violations," remarked one panelist, reflecting the sentiments of the group. "By promoting fair and ethical trade practices, we can create an environment where human rights are respected and protected."

The story then transitioned to a workshop on corporate social responsibility, where participants shared best practices and innovative strategies for promoting human rights in the context of trade and investment. Discussions focused on issues such as supply chain transparency, responsible sourcing, and community engagement.

"Businesses have a responsibility to respect human rights throughout their operations and value chains," Minister Mukwiza affirmed, her voice filled with conviction. "By promoting corporate social responsibility, we can ensure that trade contributes to the advancement of human rights and social justice."

Back at the Human Rights Council, participants reflected on the discussions and insights shared throughout the event. The hall buzzed with energy as they exchanged ideas and forged new partnerships to advance the cause of trade and human rights.

Minister Mukwiza and her delegation shared a moment of satisfaction, knowing that their contributions had helped to shape the global dialogue on trade and human rights considerations. The council had been a testament to the importance of integrating human rights principles into trade policies, and they were inspired to continue their efforts in promoting a more just and equitable world for all.

Chapter 6: International Financial Architecture

6.1 The Role of International Financial Institutions (IFIs)

Minister of Finance Peter Lumamba, alongside esteemed delegates, entered the grand halls of the G20 Summit in Washington D.C. The atmosphere was charged with anticipation as representatives from the world's largest economies gathered to discuss the role of International Financial Institutions (IFIs) in shaping the global financial landscape.

"International Financial Institutions play a crucial role in promoting financial stability and fostering economic development," Minister Lumamba declared, his voice echoing in the expansive summit hall. "Let us explore how we can strengthen the role of IFIs to address the challenges of the 21st century."

The setting transitioned to the summit stage, where Minister Lumamba stood before a distinguished audience of world leaders, economists, and financial experts. The flags of the G20 nations fluttered in the background, symbolizing the unity of purpose in addressing global financial issues.

"International Financial Institutions, including the IMF, World Bank, and regional development banks, play a vital role in providing financial assistance, technical expertise, and policy advice to member countries," Minister Lumamba began, capturing the attention of the audience. "By working together and leveraging the expertise of IFIs, we can build a more resilient and inclusive global financial architecture."

The narrative shifted to a panel discussion, where experts explored the diverse functions and roles of International Financial Institutions. Discussions ranged from crisis prevention and resolution to poverty alleviation and sustainable development.

"IFIs serve as critical sources of financing and knowledge for countries facing economic challenges," remarked one panelist, echoing the sentiments of the group. "By promoting transparency, accountability, and good governance, IFIs can help countries achieve their development goals and overcome financial vulnerabilities."

The story then transitioned to a workshop on IFI reforms, where participants shared best practices and innovative ideas for enhancing the effectiveness and responsiveness of International Financial Institutions. Discussions focused on issues such as governance reforms, lending practices, and the alignment of IFI policies with global development priorities.

"IFI reforms are essential for ensuring that these institutions remain relevant and responsive to the evolving needs of member countries," Minister Lumamba affirmed, his voice filled with determination. "By fostering greater inclusivity and transparency, we can strengthen the legitimacy and effectiveness of IFIs in promoting global financial stability and sustainable development."

Back at the G20 Summit, participants reflected on the discussions and insights shared throughout the event. The halls buzzed with energy as they exchanged ideas and forged new partnerships to advance the cause of international financial cooperation.

Minister Lumamba and his delegation shared a moment of satisfaction, knowing that their contributions had helped to shape the global dialogue on the role of International Financial Institutions. The summit had been a testament to the importance of IFIs in promoting financial stability and fostering economic development, and they were inspired to continue their efforts in building a more resilient and inclusive global financial architecture for the benefit of all.

6.2 International Monetary Fund (IMF) Programs and Conditionality

Minister of Finance Peter Lumamba, accompanied by his advisors, entered the impressive halls of the International Monetary Fund (IMF) headquarters in Washington D.C. The atmosphere was solemn as they prepared to discuss the intricacies of IMF programs and conditionality.

"IMF programs are crucial for countries facing economic challenges, but they also come with conditions that can be contentious," Minister Lumamba declared, his voice echoing in the grand corridors of the IMF building. "Let us explore how we can navigate IMF programs and conditionality to promote sustainable development and protect national interests."

The setting transitioned to the IMF boardroom, where

Minister Lumamba and his delegation sat across the table from IMF officials. Tension hung in the air as they delved into discussions about the terms and conditions of an IMF program for their country.

"IMF programs often require countries to implement difficult economic reforms in exchange for financial assistance," remarked one IMF official, reflecting the stance of the institution. "These reforms are necessary to restore macroeconomic stability and promote long-term growth."

The narrative shifted to a negotiation session, where Minister Lumamba and his team engaged in intense discussions with IMF representatives. They debated the feasibility and implications of the proposed reforms, advocating for adjustments to safeguard national interests and protect vulnerable populations.

"As representatives of our country, it is our duty to ensure that IMF programs are aligned with our development priorities and do not exacerbate social inequalities," Minister Lumamba asserted, his voice firm and unwavering. "We are committed to implementing reforms that promote sustainable development and protect the well-being of our citizens."

The story then transitioned to a public forum on IMF conditionality, where civil society organizations, academics, and citizens gathered to voice their concerns and perspectives. Emotions ran high as participants shared their experiences and opinions on the impact of IMF programs on their lives and communities.

"IMF conditionality must be transparent, accountable, and sensitive to the needs of affected populations," remarked one participant, echoing the sentiments of many. "It is essential to ensure that IMF programs promote social justice and human rights, rather than exacerbating inequalities and hardships."

Back at the IMF headquarters, Minister Lumamba and his delegation reflected on the discussions and negotiations they had participated in. The corridors buzzed with energy as they exchanged ideas and forged new partnerships to advocate for more equitable and sustainable IMF programs.

Minister Lumamba reaffirmed his commitment to promoting national interests and protecting the well-being of his citizens in the face of IMF conditionality. The discussions had been challenging, but they had laid the groundwork for a more constructive and inclusive dialogue on the role of the IMF in promoting global financial stability and sustainable development.

6.3 World Bank Group Initiatives and Development Financing

Minister of Finance Peter Lumamba, flanked by his advisors, stepped into the bustling corridors of the World Bank Headquarters in Washington D.C. The air was charged with anticipation as they prepared to discuss the World Bank Group's initiatives and development financing.

"The World Bank Group plays a pivotal role in providing development assistance and financing to countries around the world," Minister Lumamba declared, his voice resonating in the grand halls of the World Bank building. "Let us explore how we can leverage World Bank initiatives to promote inclusive and sustainable development."

The setting transitioned to the World Bank boardroom, where Minister Lumamba and his delegation sat across the table from World Bank officials. The mood was serious as they delved into discussions about the World Bank's financing programs and initiatives.

"The World Bank Group is committed to supporting countries in their efforts to achieve sustainable development goals," remarked one World Bank official, reflecting the institution's mission. "We offer a range of financial products and technical assistance to address development challenges and promote inclusive growth."

The narrative shifted to a strategy session, where Minister Lumamba and his team strategized on how best to utilize World Bank financing to address key development priorities in their country. They discussed potential projects and initiatives that could leverage World Bank support to drive economic growth and poverty reduction.

"We must ensure that World Bank financing aligns with our national development agenda and priorities," Minister Lumamba asserted, his voice filled with determination. "By targeting investments in critical sectors such as infrastructure, education, and healthcare, we can lay the foundation for long-term sustainable development."

The story then transitioned to a consultation with civil society organizations, where representatives from grassroots movements and community groups shared their perspectives on World Bank initiatives and development financing. Emotions ran high as participants advocated for greater transparency, accountability, and community involvement in World Bank-funded projects.

"The World Bank must engage with local communities and ensure that their voices are heard in the decision-making process," remarked one civil society leader, echoing the sentiments of many. "Development financing should prioritize the needs and aspirations of the people it seeks to serve."

Back at the World Bank headquarters, Minister Lumamba and his delegation reflected on the discussions and consultations they had participated in. The corridors buzzed with energy as they exchanged ideas and forged new partnerships to advocate for more transparent, accountable, and community-driven World Bank initiatives.

Minister Lumamba reaffirmed his commitment to leveraging World Bank financing to drive inclusive and sustainable development in his country. The discussions had been fruitful, laying the groundwork for a more collaborative and impactful partnership between his government and the World Bank Group in pursuit of shared development goals.

6.4 Regional Development Banks and Financial Assistance

Minister of Finance Peter Lumamba, accompanied by his delegation, arrived at the imposing headquarters of the African Development Bank (AfDB) in Abidjan. The atmosphere was filled with anticipation as they prepared to discuss the role of regional development banks in providing financial assistance and promoting development in Africa.

"The regional development banks are vital institutions that play a crucial role in supporting the economic growth and development of our region," Minister Lumamba declared, his voice echoing in the spacious halls of the AfDB headquarters. "Let us explore how we can leverage their resources and expertise to address the development challenges facing our continent."

The setting transitioned to the AfDB conference room, where

CHAPTER 6: INTERNATIONAL FINANCIAL ARCHITECTURE

Minister Lumamba and his delegation sat down for discussions with AfDB officials. The mood was serious as they delved into the various financing instruments and programs offered by the AfDB to support development projects across Africa.

"The AfDB is committed to financing projects that promote sustainable development, inclusive growth, and poverty reduction in Africa," remarked one AfDB official, outlining the institution's mandate. "We offer a range of financial products and technical assistance to address the diverse needs of our member countries."

The narrative shifted to a consultation with regional leaders, where representatives from African countries gathered to discuss their priorities and perspectives on AfDB assistance. Emotions ran high as participants shared their aspirations and challenges, highlighting the importance of tailored solutions to address Africa's unique development context.

"The AfDB must prioritize investments in critical sectors such as infrastructure, agriculture, and human capital development to unlock Africa's full potential," remarked one regional leader, echoing the sentiments of many. "Development assistance should be aligned with our national priorities and contribute to the achievement of sustainable development goals."

The story then transitioned to a field visit to AfDB-funded projects, where Minister Lumamba and his delegation had the opportunity to see firsthand the impact of AfDB assistance on the ground. They visited infrastructure projects, agricultural initiatives, and education programs, meeting with local communities and project beneficiaries along the way.

"These projects are transforming lives and communities, empowering people to build a better future for themselves and their children," Minister Lumamba remarked, deeply moved by the sights and stories he encountered. "The AfDB's support is instrumental in driving sustainable development and prosperity across Africa."

Back at the AfDB headquarters, Minister Lumamba and his delegation reflected on the discussions and experiences they had during their visit. The corridors buzzed with energy as they exchanged ideas and forged new partnerships to leverage AfDB assistance for the benefit of their country and the continent as a whole.

Minister Lumamba reaffirmed his commitment to working closely with the AfDB and other regional development banks to address Africa's development challenges and unlock its full potential. The discussions had been enlightening, laying the groundwork for a more collaborative and impactful partnership between his government and the AfDB in pursuit of shared development objectives.

6.5 Sovereign Debt Restructuring and Debt Relief Initiatives

Minister of Finance Peter Lumamba, flanked by his advisors, entered the United Nations conference room in New York City. The atmosphere was tense as representatives from debtor and creditor nations gathered to discuss sovereign debt restructuring and debt relief initiatives.

"Sovereign debt burdens can cripple countries and hinder their development prospects," Minister Lumamba declared, his voice echoing in the cavernous room. "Let us explore how we can address the challenges of unsustainable debt and promote debt relief initiatives that enable countries to achieve their development goals."

The setting transitioned to the negotiation table, where Minister Lumamba and his delegation sat across from representatives of creditor nations and international financial institutions. Tensions ran high as they grappled with the complexities of sovereign debt restructuring and the terms of debt relief initiatives.

"Sovereign debt restructuring must be approached in a fair, transparent, and sustainable manner," Minister Lumamba asserted, his voice unwavering. "We must work together to find solutions that alleviate the burden on debtor nations while ensuring the interests of creditors are respected."

The narrative shifted to a consultation with civil society organizations, where representatives from grassroots movements and advocacy groups voiced their perspectives on sovereign debt restructuring and debt relief. Emotions ran high as participants shared stories of the human toll of unsustainable debt burdens and called for greater transparency and accountability in debt management processes.

"Debt relief initiatives must prioritize the needs and well-being of affected populations," remarked one civil society leader, echoing the sentiments of many. "It is essential to involve civil society in decision-making processes and ensure that debt restructuring efforts promote social justice and human rights."

The story then transitioned to a roundtable discussion on innovative financing mechanisms, where experts explored alternative approaches to debt restructuring and debt relief. Discussions ranged from debt-for-nature swaps to diaspora bonds and social impact bonds, offering new perspectives on addressing debt challenges.

"Innovative financing mechanisms offer promising solutions for addressing sovereign debt burdens and promoting sustainable development," Minister Lumamba remarked, inspired by the ideas and insights shared during the discussion. "We must explore new avenues for financing development and breaking the cycle of debt dependency."

Back at the United Nations headquarters, Minister Lumamba and his delegation reflected on the discussions and consultations they had participated in. The corridors buzzed with energy as they exchanged ideas and forged new partnerships to advocate for more equitable and sustainable approaches to sovereign debt restructuring and debt relief.

Minister Lumamba reaffirmed his commitment to working collaboratively with all stakeholders to address the challenges of unsustainable debt and promote inclusive development. The discussions had been challenging, but they had laid the groundwork for a more constructive and effective dialogue on sovereign debt management and debt relief initiatives, paving the way for a brighter future for debtor nations and their citizens.

6.6 Emerging Trends in Global Financial Governance

Minister of Finance Peter Lumamba, seated in front of his computer screen, joined the virtual IMF Annual Meeting from his office. The digital interface buzzed with activity as policymakers, economists, and financial experts from around the world convened to discuss emerging trends in global financial governance.

"The landscape of global financial governance is rapidly evolving, driven by technological advancements, geopolitical shifts, and changing economic dynamics," Minister Lumamba remarked, his voice projecting through the virtual conference platform. "Let us explore the emerging trends shaping the future of international financial architecture."

The setting transitioned to a panel discussion on digital finance and financial technology (fintech), where experts explored the transformative potential of digital innovations in reshaping the financial landscape. Discussions ranged from digital payments and blockchain technology to artificial intelligence and cybersecurity.

"The rise of digital finance and fintech presents both opportunities and challenges for global financial governance," remarked one panelist, reflecting the sentiments of the group. "It is essential to strike a balance between innovation and regulation to harness the benefits of digitalization while safeguarding financial stability and consumer protection."

The narrative shifted to a workshop on sustainable finance and environmental, social, and governance (ESG) investing, where participants discussed the growing importance of sustainability considerations in investment decisions. Discussions focused on issues such as green bonds, impact investing, and corporate responsibility.

"Sustainable finance is gaining momentum as investors increasingly recognize the importance of integrating ESG factors into their decision-making processes," Minister Lumamba affirmed, his voice resonating with conviction. "By mobilizing private capital towards sustainable development goals, we can drive positive change and build a more resilient and inclusive global economy."

The story then transitioned to a roundtable discussion on multilateral cooperation, where policymakers and diplomats explored the role of international institutions in addressing global economic challenges. Discussions ranged from trade tensions and geopolitical rivalries to the need for greater coordination in crisis response and economic recovery efforts.

"Multilateral cooperation is more important than ever in navigating today's complex and interconnected global economy," remarked one participant, emphasizing the importance of solidarity and collaboration in addressing common challenges. "We must strengthen international institutions and uphold the principles of multilateralism to build a more stable, prosperous, and inclusive world for all."

Back at the virtual IMF Annual Meeting, participants reflected on the discussions and insights shared throughout the conference. The digital platform buzzed with energy as they exchanged ideas and forged new partnerships to advance the cause of global financial governance.

Minister Lumamba and his delegation shared a moment of satisfaction, knowing that their contributions had helped to shape the global dialogue on emerging trends in international financial architecture. The conference had been a testament to the dynamic nature of global finance and the importance of adaptation and cooperation in addressing the challenges and opportunities of the 21st century.

7

Chapter 7: Trade Policy Analysis and Evaluation

7.1 Quantitative Methods in Trade Policy Analysis

Professor Anna, an esteemed economist, stood at the front of a university classroom filled with eager students. The whiteboard behind her was covered in equations and graphs, illustrating the complexities of trade policy analysis.

"Today, we delve into the quantitative methods used to analyze and evaluate trade policies," Professor Anna announced, her voice commanding attention. "Let us explore how these methods provide valuable insights into the impacts of trade policies on economies, industries, and households."

The setting transitioned to Professor Anna delivering a lecture on trade models, where she explained the intricacies of computable general equilibrium (CGE) models and gravity models. With enthusiasm, she illustrated how these models simulate the effects of trade policies on key economic variables such as GDP, employment, and income distribution.

"Trade models provide a comprehensive framework for analyzing the effects of trade policies under various scenarios," Professor Anna explained, her passion for the subject evident in her animated gestures. "By capturing the interdependencies between sectors and regions, these models help policymakers make informed decisions that promote economic growth and welfare."

The narrative shifted to a workshop on data analysis, where students were immersed in the practical application of quantitative methods in trade policy analysis. Armed with laptops and datasets, they explored techniques such as regression analysis, input-output analysis, and computable general equilibrium modeling.

"Data analysis is essential for assessing the impact of trade policies on different stakeholders," remarked one student, as they delved into the intricacies of econometric techniques. "By analyzing trade data and economic indicators, we can identify patterns and trends that inform policy decisions and strategies."

The story then transitioned to a group discussion, where students engaged in lively debates on various trade policy scenarios. They examined the potential effects of trade liberalization, protectionism, and regional integration on domestic industries, employment levels, and consumer welfare.

"As future economists, it is our responsibility to critically evaluate trade policies and their implications for society," remarked one student, as they defended their policy recommendations based on quantitative analysis. "By rigorously assessing trade policies using quantitative methods, we can contribute to evidence-based policymaking and economic development."

Back in the university classroom, Professor Anna and her

students reflected on the day's discussions and insights. The room buzzed with energy as they exchanged ideas and reflected on the importance of quantitative methods in trade policy analysis.

Professor Anna reaffirmed her commitment to equipping her students with the analytical tools and skills needed to navigate the complexities of trade policy analysis. The discussions had been enlightening, laying the groundwork for a new generation of economists ready to tackle the challenges of global trade and economic policy with rigor and expertise.

7.2 Trade Policy Instruments and Their Effects

Minister of Finance Peter Lumamba, surrounded by his directors and advisors, convened a high-level meeting in the ministerial conference room in Lusaka. The topic of the day was the evaluation of various trade policy instruments and their potential effects on Zambia's economy.

"Today, we must scrutinize the trade policy instruments at our disposal and assess their impacts on our economy," Minister Lumamba declared, setting the stage for an intense discussion. "Our goal is to identify the most effective measures to promote economic growth and development while protecting our domestic industries."

The setting transitioned to a detailed presentation by Dr. Miriam Zulu, the Director of Trade Policy. With a laser pointer in hand, she highlighted key points on a projection screen filled with data and graphs on tariffs and quotas.

"Tariffs and quotas are among the most commonly used trade policy instruments," Dr. Zulu explained, her voice confident and clear. "While tariffs can generate government revenue and protect domestic industries, they can also lead to higher prices for consumers and retaliatory measures from trading partners. Quotas, on the other hand, directly limit the quantity of imports, potentially reducing market access for foreign producers but ensuring market stability for local industries."

The narrative shifted to a lively discussion on subsidies and export incentives. The room buzzed with activity as advisors debated the merits and drawbacks of these instruments, drawing from recent case studies and economic reports.

"Subsidies can boost the competitiveness of our domestic industries, especially in agriculture and manufacturing," remarked one advisor, citing examples from other countries. "However, we must be cautious of the fiscal burden they impose and the potential for trade disputes if subsidies are perceived as unfair trade practices."

"Export incentives, such as tax rebates and financial support for exporters, can help diversify our export base and penetrate new markets," added another advisor. "These measures can drive economic growth, but we must ensure they align with international trade rules and our long-term development strategy."

The story then transitioned to a scenario analysis session, where the team examined the potential effects of entering new trade agreements. They used advanced economic models to simulate the impacts on various sectors of the Zambian economy.

"Trade agreements can open new markets for our goods and services, fostering economic integration and cooperation," Minister Lumamba noted, reviewing the projections. "However, they also require us to carefully consider the concessions we make and the adjustments needed to enhance our competitiveness."

Back in the ministerial conference room, Minister Lumamba and his team reflected on the day's discussions and analyses. The room buzzed with energy as they exchanged ideas and forged new strategies to optimize the use of trade policy instruments.

Minister Lumamba reaffirmed his commitment to leveraging trade policy instruments effectively to achieve Zambia's development goals. The discussions had been rigorous, laying the groundwork for a more strategic and informed approach to trade policy that balanced the needs of domestic industries with the opportunities of the global market.

7.3 Trade Liberalization and Economic Growth

The National Economic Forum was in full swing, held in the grand ballroom of Lusaka's premier conference center. The audience comprised government officials, business leaders, economists, and representatives from international organizations. Minister of Finance Peter Lumamba stood at the podium, ready to address the key topic of the day the impact of trade liberalization on economic growth.

"Ladies and gentlemen, today we discuss one of the most pivotal aspects of our economic policy—trade liberalization," Minister Lumamba began, his voice carrying the weight of both optimism and caution. "We need to understand how opening our markets can drive economic growth, create jobs, and improve living standards while also considering the risks and challenges it poses."

Scene Transition Expert Panel on Trade Liberalization

The setting transitioned to an expert panel discussion featuring renowned economists and trade policy experts. Dr. Henry Banda, an economist known for his extensive research on trade liberalization, took the floor.

"Trade liberalization involves reducing tariffs, eliminating quotas, and dismantling other trade barriers," Dr. Banda explained. "This process can lead to increased competition, efficiency gains, and access to a broader range of goods and services. However, it also requires economies to be resilient and adaptable to external shocks."

The narrative shifted to a presentation on case studies from countries that have undergone trade liberalization. Charts and graphs illustrated the economic trajectories of nations like South Korea, Vietnam, and Chile.

"South Korea's rapid industrialization was significantly driven by trade liberalization policies," noted the presenter, pointing to a graph showing a sharp rise in GDP growth following liberalization measures. "These countries harnessed the benefits of open markets to boost exports, attract foreign investment, and spur innovation."

The story then transitioned to a roundtable discussion where Zambian business leaders shared their perspectives on trade liberalization. The atmosphere was one of cautious optimism as they discussed the potential for growth and the need for supportive policies.

"Trade liberalization offers immense opportunities for our businesses to expand into new markets," remarked a leading textile manufacturer. "However, we need adequate infrastructure, access to finance, and capacity-building initiatives to compete effectively on the global stage."

"Protecting nascent industries while gradually opening up the market is crucial," added another business leader from the agriculture sector. "We must ensure that our farmers and local producers are not overwhelmed by sudden influxes of foreign competition."

The narrative shifted to a town hall meeting where local community members voiced their concerns and hopes regarding trade liberalization. Emotions ran high as citizens discussed the potential impacts on employment, prices, and social welfare.

"We need to ensure that the benefits of trade liberalization reach everyone, not just big businesses," a young entrepreneur emphasized. "Small and medium enterprises should receive support to scale up and take advantage of new market opportunities."

Back at the National Economic Forum, Minister Lumamba wrapped up the discussions, summarizing the key takeaways from the expert panel, business leaders, and community members.

"Trade liberalization is a powerful tool for economic growth, but it must be implemented thoughtfully and strategically," Minister Lumamba concluded. "By balancing openness with protective measures, investing in infrastructure, and supporting local industries, we can harness the benefits of trade liberalization to drive sustainable development and prosperity for all Zambians."

The forum ended with a renewed sense of purpose and commitment, setting the stage for Zambia's future trade policy that would navigate the complex dynamics of global markets while fostering inclusive growth and development at home.

7.4 Impact Assessment of Trade Agreements

Minister of Finance Peter Lumamba, along with his team of directors and advisors, gathered in the conference room at the Ministry of Finance. The agenda was to assess the potential impacts of proposed trade agreements on Zambia's economy. The room was filled with documents, laptops, and projection screens displaying various economic models and data sets.

"We are at a critical juncture," Minister Lumamba began, addressing the room. "It's essential that we thoroughly analyze the implications of entering new trade agreements to ensure they align with our national development goals and protect our economic interests."

The setting transitioned to a detailed presentation by Chief Economic Analyst, Dr. Chisala Mumba. Using a combination of charts, graphs, and statistical models, she illustrated the potential economic impacts of the proposed trade agreements with regional and global partners.

"Trade agreements can significantly influence our trade balance, employment rates, and GDP growth," Dr. Mumba explained, pointing to a graph showing projected economic outcomes. "Our analysis focuses on both the short-term adjustments and long-term benefits, including increased market access, technology transfer, and foreign direct investment."

The narrative shifted to a focused discussion on sectoral impacts. Various directors presented their findings on how different sectors, such as agriculture, manufacturing, and services, might be affected by the trade agreements.

"The agriculture sector could benefit from reduced tariffs and increased market access," noted the Director of Agriculture, Ms. Lillian Banda. "However, we must consider the need for capacity building and infrastructure development to support our farmers in scaling up production and meeting international standards."

"In the manufacturing sector, there is potential for growth through partnerships and technology transfer," added Mr. Patrick Mwale, Director of Industry. "Yet, we must also protect our nascent industries from being outcompeted by established foreign companies. Strategic support and gradual liberalization are key."

The story then transitioned to a consultation with representatives from trade partner countries. The room was filled with diplomats and trade negotiators, engaging in spirited discussions about the terms and conditions of the proposed agreements.

"Mutual benefits and equitable terms are crucial for successful trade agreements," emphasized one trade negotiator from a partner country. "We are committed to fostering a partnership that supports economic growth and development for all parties involved."

"Transparency and inclusivity in the negotiation process will build trust and ensure the agreements are beneficial to both sides," echoed another diplomat. "Let's work together to identify areas of common interest and address potential concerns."

The narrative shifted to a community feedback session where local business owners, workers, and civil society representatives voiced their concerns and expectations regarding the trade agreements. Emotions were high as participants shared their perspectives on how the agreements might impact their lives and livelihoods.

"Trade agreements should create opportunities for local

businesses and workers, not just large corporations," asserted a small business owner. "We need assurances that the benefits will trickle down to the grassroots level."

"Environmental and social standards must be upheld in these agreements," added a representative from a local NGO. "We cannot compromise on sustainability and the well-being of our communities."

Back in the conference room, Minister Lumamba and his team synthesized the insights from their analyses, consultations, and community feedback. The atmosphere was one of cautious optimism as they prepared to finalize their recommendations.

"Trade agreements have the potential to drive economic growth and development, but they must be crafted carefully to ensure broad-based benefits and mitigate potential risks," Minister Lumamba concluded. "Our assessment underscores the importance of strategic planning, stakeholder engagement, and continuous monitoring to maximize the positive impacts of these agreements."

The team left the meeting with a renewed sense of purpose, ready to navigate the complexities of trade policy and forge agreements that would support Zambia's journey towards sustainable and inclusive economic growth.

7.5 Trade Dispute Resolution Mechanisms

The grand hall of the International Trade Conference in Geneva was abuzz with activity. Delegates from around the world gathered to discuss and negotiate trade issues. Minister of Finance Peter Lumamba, along with his legal advisor, Ms. Joyce Tembo, was in attendance, representing Zambia's interests.

"Today, we focus on the mechanisms for resolving trade disputes," Minister Lumamba announced, addressing a gathering of international delegates. "Effective dispute resolution is crucial for maintaining fair and stable international trade relations."

The setting transitioned to a panel discussion featuring experts in international trade law and representatives from the World Trade Organization (WTO). Dr. Hans Weber, a renowned trade lawyer, began by outlining the core principles of trade dispute resolution mechanisms.

"The WTO's Dispute Settlement Understanding (DSU) is the backbone of international trade dispute resolution," Dr. Weber explained. "It provides a structured process for resolving conflicts between member states, ensuring that disputes are settled based on agreed rules and legal principles."

The narrative shifted to a case study analysis of a recent trade dispute between two countries over agricultural subsidies. The room was filled with legal documents, precedents, and evidence as Ms. Tembo guided the team through the complexities of the case.

"This dispute highlights the importance of adhering to international trade rules and the role of the WTO in ensuring compliance," Ms. Tembo remarked. "Through arbitration and adjudication, we can resolve such conflicts and uphold the integrity of the global trading system."

The story then transitioned to a simulation of a trade dispute hearing at the WTO headquarters. Minister Lumamba and his team participated in a mock arbitration process, presenting their arguments and evidence before a panel of judges.

"We argue that the subsidies provided by the respondent country distort trade and unfairly disadvantage our domestic producers," Minister Lumamba asserted, presenting a detailed report. "We seek remedial action to level the playing field and restore fair competition."

The opposing counsel responded with counterarguments, defending their country's policies and highlighting their adherence to trade agreements. The judges listened intently, asking probing questions and examining the evidence presented by both sides.

The narrative shifted to a bilateral negotiation session where Minister Lumamba and Ms. Tembo engaged in direct talks with their counterparts from the opposing country. The atmosphere was tense but constructive as they sought a mutually agreeable solution.

"Let us find a way to resolve this dispute amicably," Minister Lumamba proposed, his tone conciliatory yet firm. "We believe in the value of maintaining strong trade relations and are willing to explore compromise solutions that respect both parties' interests."

After hours of negotiation, they reached a tentative agreement involving phased adjustments to the disputed subsidies and increased cooperation in agricultural trade.

Back at the International Trade Conference, Minister Lumamba and Ms. Tembo shared their experiences and insights with other delegates. The atmosphere was one of collaboration and mutual learning as they reflected on the importance of effective dispute resolution mechanisms.

"Trade disputes are inevitable in a complex and interconnected global economy," Minister Lumamba concluded. "But with robust mechanisms for resolution, we can ensure that conflicts are managed fairly and efficiently, promoting stability and trust in the international trading system."

The conference ended with a renewed commitment to strengthening dispute resolution processes and fostering a more equitable and transparent global trade environment. Minister Lumamba and his team returned to Zambia, ready to implement the lessons learned and contribute to a more resilient and fair international trade system.

7.6 Trade Policy Formulation and Implementation Challenges

The Ministry of Finance's main conference room was filled with senior officials and advisors, all focused on the challenges of formulating and implementing effective trade policies. Minister Peter Lumamba sat at the head of the table, ready to lead the discussion.

"Colleagues, today we address the formidable challenges we face in formulating and implementing our trade policies," Minister Lumamba began. "It's crucial that we understand these obstacles to devise strategies that will help us overcome them."

The setting transitioned to a presentation by Mr. Thomas Nkosi, the Director of Trade Policy. He highlighted several critical issues that hinder effective policy formulation.

"One major challenge is aligning our trade policies with national development goals," Mr. Nkosi explained, pointing to a flowchart on the screen. "Balancing the interests of various sectors, such as agriculture, manufacturing, and services, often leads to conflicting priorities."

"Additionally," he continued, "we must consider the influence of external factors like global market trends, regional trade agreements, and international trade regulations. These factors can complicate our efforts to create cohesive and effective policies."

The narrative shifted to a roundtable discussion where various directors shared their experiences and insights on the challenges of implementing trade policies.

"Implementation requires robust institutional capacity and coordination among various government agencies," remarked Ms. Joyce Tembo, Director of Legal Affairs. "However, bureaucratic inefficiencies and lack of resources often impede our progress."

"Moreover, enforcement of trade regulations and standards is critical," added Mr. Patrick Mwale, Director of Industry. "Without proper monitoring and compliance mechanisms, our policies cannot achieve their intended outcomes."

The story then transitioned to a stakeholder consultation meeting, where representatives from the private sector, civil society, and academia shared their perspectives on the challenges they face in the implementation of trade policies.

"As business owners, we often struggle with the unpredictability of trade policy changes," said a prominent business leader. "Frequent amendments and lack of clear communication from the government create uncertainty and hinder our ability to plan and invest."

"From a civil society standpoint, ensuring that trade policies are inclusive and consider the impacts on vulnerable communities is a significant challenge," added a representative from an NGO. "We need more transparent and participatory processes to address these concerns."

The narrative shifted to a field visit where Minister Lumamba and his team inspected a busy border trade post. They observed firsthand the logistical challenges and bottlenecks that traders and customs officials faced daily.

"Efficient border management is crucial for the smooth implementation of our trade policies," Minister Lumamba noted, speaking with customs officials and traders. "Addressing these on-ground challenges is essential for facilitating trade and ensuring policy effectiveness."

Back in the Ministry of Finance conference room, the team regrouped to reflect on the insights gained from their discussions and field visits. The atmosphere was one of determination and collaboration as they strategized on overcoming the identified challenges.

"To formulate and implement effective trade policies, we need a comprehensive approach that addresses institutional, logistical, and stakeholder-related challenges," Minister Lumamba concluded. "By enhancing our institutional capacities, improving coordination, and fostering inclusive dialogue, we can create policies that drive economic growth and development."

The meeting ended with a renewed sense of purpose and commitment. The team was ready to tackle the complexities of trade policy formulation and implementation, armed with a deeper understanding of the challenges and a clear vision for the future.

8

Chapter 8: Public Finance in Global Context

8.1 International Taxation and Tax Harmonization

The grand auditorium of the International Tax Conference in Brussels was filled with delegates from countries around the world. Minister of Finance Peter Lumamba, accompanied by his tax policy advisor, Mr. David Chanda, took their seats among the attendees. The topic of the day international taxation and tax harmonization.

"Welcome, esteemed delegates, to the International Tax Conference," announced the conference moderator. "Today, we delve into the complexities of international taxation and explore avenues for tax harmonization to address global tax challenges."

Minister Lumamba stood at the podium, addressing the audience with authority and conviction. His words echoed through the hall, capturing the attention of all present.

"Ladies and gentlemen, in an increasingly interconnected

world, the need for international tax cooperation has never been greater," Minister Lumamba declared. "We must work together to ensure that our tax systems are fair, transparent, and effective in generating revenue for public goods and services."

The setting transitioned to an expert panel discussion featuring leading tax policy experts and representatives from international organizations. They engaged in a lively exchange of ideas on the benefits and challenges of tax harmonization.

"Tax harmonization can promote fairness and reduce tax evasion and avoidance," remarked a renowned tax economist. "However, achieving harmonization requires coordination among countries with diverse tax systems and priorities."

The narrative shifted to a case study presentation on the European Union's efforts towards tax harmonization. Charts and graphs illustrated the evolution of tax policies and the impact of harmonization initiatives on member states.

"The European Union's journey towards tax harmonization offers valuable lessons for global cooperation," noted the presenter. "By aligning tax rules and combating harmful tax practices, member states have fostered economic integration and strengthened the single market."

The story then transitioned to a roundtable discussion where finance ministers from various countries exchanged views and experiences on international taxation and tax harmonization. Minister Lumamba shared Zambia's perspective on the challenges and opportunities in this area.

"Tax harmonization requires careful consideration of national interests and sovereignty," Minister Lumamba emphasized. "However, we recognize the benefits of cooperation in combating tax evasion, promoting investment, and ensuring a level playing field for businesses."

The narrative shifted to bilateral meetings where Minister Lumamba and Mr. Chanda engaged in discussions with counterparts from other countries on tax treaties and agreements. They explored areas of mutual interest and exchanged proposals for enhancing cooperation on tax matters.

"Our tax treaties should reflect the realities of the modern global economy," Minister Lumamba asserted during the meetings. "They must strike a balance between preventing double taxation and preventing tax avoidance and evasion."

Back at the International Tax Conference, Minister Lumamba and Mr. Chanda reflected on the day's discussions and insights. The atmosphere was one of optimism and determination as they prepared to return to Zambia and continue their efforts towards international tax cooperation and harmonization.

"As we navigate the complexities of international taxation, let us remain committed to the principles of fairness, transparency, and cooperation," Minister Lumamba concluded. "Together, we can build a more equitable and sustainable global tax system that benefits all."

The conference ended with a renewed sense of purpose, as delegates departed with a shared commitment to advancing international tax cooperation and harmonization for the benefit of the global community.

8.2 Cross-Border Financial Flows and Capital Controls

Minister of Finance Peter Lumamba, accompanied by his economic advisor, Ms. Sarah Banda, entered the prestigious halls of the International Monetary Fund headquarters. They

CHAPTER 8: PUBLIC FINANCE IN GLOBAL CONTEXT

were there to attend a high-level summit on cross-border financial flows and capital controls.

"Welcome, Minister Lumamba, to the IMF summit on cross-border financial flows," greeted the summit organizer as they entered the conference room. "Today, we delve into the complexities of managing capital flows and the role of capital controls in safeguarding financial stability."

Minister Lumamba took the podium, his presence commanding attention as he addressed the audience of international policymakers, economists, and financial experts.

"Ladies and gentlemen, in an era of unprecedented global financial integration, the management of cross-border financial flows is of paramount importance," Minister Lumamba began, his voice resonating with authority. "We must strike a delicate balance between promoting financial openness and safeguarding against the risks of excessive volatility and instability."

The setting transitioned to an expert panel discussion featuring leading economists and central bank governors. They engaged in a robust exchange of ideas on the challenges posed by cross-border financial flows and the effectiveness of capital controls in managing these flows.

"Capital flows can bring significant benefits, including access to investment and financial diversification," remarked a renowned economist. "However, they can also pose risks, such as currency volatility, asset bubbles, and financial contagion."

The narrative shifted to a case study presentation on a country's experience with implementing capital controls during a period of financial turbulence. The presenter highlighted the rationale behind the controls, their impact on the economy, and lessons learned for future policy decisions.

"During times of crisis, capital controls can help mitigate the adverse effects of speculative capital inflows and outflows," explained the presenter. "However, their effectiveness depends on careful design, coordination with other macroeconomic policies, and clear communication with market participants."

The story then transitioned to a roundtable discussion where finance ministers from various countries shared their perspectives and experiences with cross-border financial flows and capital controls. Minister Lumamba contributed Zambia's insights and challenges in managing capital flows.

"As a developing economy, Zambia faces unique challenges in managing capital flows," Minister Lumamba stated during the discussion. "While we recognize the benefits of financial openness, we must also ensure that our financial system remains stable and resilient to external shocks."

The narrative shifted to bilateral meetings where Minister Lumamba and Ms. Banda engaged in discussions with counterparts from other countries on financial regulation and supervision. They explored avenues for enhancing cooperation and coordination in managing cross-border financial flows.

"Effective financial regulation and supervision are essential for maintaining financial stability and investor confidence," Minister Lumamba emphasized during the meetings. "We must work together to strengthen our regulatory frameworks and exchange best practices in this area."

Back at the IMF headquarters, Minister Lumamba and Ms. Banda reflected on the day's discussions and insights. The atmosphere was one of determination and collaboration as they prepared to return to Zambia and continue their efforts to manage cross-border financial flows and promote financial stability.

"As we navigate the complexities of cross-border financial flows, let us remain vigilant and proactive in safeguarding our financial system," Minister Lumamba concluded. "By working together and learning from each other's experiences, we can build a more resilient and sustainable global financial architecture."

The summit ended with a renewed sense of purpose, as delegates departed with a shared commitment to addressing the challenges posed by cross-border financial flows and advancing policies that promote financial stability and inclusive growth.

8.3 Public-Private Partnerships (PPPs) in Infrastructure Development

Minister of Finance Peter Lumamba, accompanied by his infrastructure advisor, Mr. John Mwila, entered the bustling conference hall of the International Conference on Infrastructure Development in Singapore. The room buzzed with anticipation as delegates from across the globe gathered to discuss the role of Public-Private Partnerships (PPPs) in infrastructure development.

"Welcome, Minister Lumamba, to the International Conference on Infrastructure Development," greeted the conference organizer as they entered the auditorium. "Today, we explore innovative approaches to infrastructure financing and the transformative potential of Public-Private Partnerships."

Minister Lumamba stepped onto the stage, his presence commanding attention as he addressed the audience of policymakers, investors, and industry leaders.

"Ladies and gentlemen, infrastructure development is the cornerstone of economic growth and sustainable development,"

Minister Lumamba began, his voice resonating with conviction. "In today's rapidly evolving global landscape, Public-Private Partnerships offer a powerful mechanism for mobilizing private capital and expertise to address our infrastructure needs."

The setting transitioned to an expert panel discussion featuring leading experts in infrastructure finance and PPPs. They engaged in a dynamic dialogue on the opportunities and challenges of PPPs in infrastructure development.

"PPPs have the potential to unlock new sources of funding and innovation for infrastructure projects," remarked a prominent infrastructure financier. "However, their success depends on clear project design, risk allocation, and effective governance structures."

Scene Transition Case Study Presentation

The narrative shifted to a case study presentation on successful PPP projects from around the world. The presenter highlighted the key elements of these projects, including robust legal frameworks, transparent procurement processes, and effective risk management strategies.

"PPP projects require careful planning and execution to ensure value for money and long-term sustainability," explained the presenter. "By leveraging private sector expertise and investment, countries can accelerate infrastructure development and enhance public service delivery."

The story then transitioned to a roundtable discussion where infrastructure ministers from various countries shared their experiences and lessons learned from implementing PPPs. Minister Lumamba shared Zambia's perspective and outlined the government's commitment to promoting PPPs as a key

CHAPTER 8: PUBLIC FINANCE IN GLOBAL CONTEXT

driver of infrastructure development.

"PPPs have played a crucial role in expanding Zambia's infrastructure network and improving service delivery," Minister Lumamba stated during the discussion. "We are committed to creating an enabling environment for PPPs and attracting private sector investment in priority sectors such as energy, transportation, and water."

The narrative shifted to bilateral meetings where Minister Lumamba and Mr. Mwila engaged in discussions with potential investors and project developers interested in partnering with Zambia on infrastructure projects. They explored opportunities for collaboration and addressed investors' concerns about regulatory frameworks and project risks.

"Zambia offers attractive opportunities for infrastructure investment, with a clear pipeline of projects and a supportive policy environment," Minister Lumamba assured the investors during the meetings. "We are committed to facilitating private sector participation and ensuring the success of PPP initiatives."

Back at the conference venue, Minister Lumamba and Mr. Mwila reflected on the day's discussions and insights. The atmosphere was one of optimism and determination as they prepared to return to Zambia and continue their efforts to harness the potential of PPPs for infrastructure development.

"As we pursue our infrastructure agenda, let us embrace PPPs as a strategic tool for mobilizing resources and expertise," Minister Lumamba concluded. "By fostering partnerships between the public and private sectors, we can build the infrastructure backbone that will drive economic growth and improve the quality of life for all Zambians."

The conference ended with a renewed sense of purpose, as delegates departed with a shared commitment to advancing

PPPs as a catalyst for infrastructure development and sustainable growth around the world.

8.4 Sovereign Wealth Funds and Resource Management

Minister of Finance Peter Lumamba, accompanied by his resource management advisor, Dr. Cynthia Ng'andu, stepped into the grand hall of the International Summit on Resource Management in Dubai. The room buzzed with anticipation as delegates from resource-rich nations gathered to discuss the role of Sovereign Wealth Funds (SWFs) in resource management.

"Welcome, Minister Lumamba, to the International Summit on Resource Management," greeted the summit organizer as they entered the conference room. "Today, we explore strategies for managing natural resource wealth and leveraging Sovereign Wealth Funds for long-term economic prosperity."

Minister Lumamba took the stage, his presence commanding attention as he addressed the audience of policymakers, economists, and industry leaders.

"Ladies and gentlemen, natural resources are a blessing and a responsibility," Minister Lumamba began, his voice resonating with conviction. "As custodians of these resources, it is incumbent upon us to manage them prudently and ensure that they benefit both current and future generations."

The setting transitioned to an expert panel discussion featuring leading experts in resource management and SWFs. They engaged in a dynamic dialogue on the challenges and opportunities of managing natural resource wealth.

"Sovereign Wealth Funds can serve as powerful tools for stabilizing revenues, saving for future generations, and promoting intergenerational equity," remarked a renowned economist. "However, their success depends on clear investment strategies, transparent governance, and effective risk management."

The narrative shifted to a case study presentation on successful Sovereign Wealth Funds from around the world. The presenter highlighted the key principles that underpin these funds, including transparency, accountability, and alignment with national development goals.

"Successful Sovereign Wealth Funds prioritize long-term value creation and sustainable development," explained the presenter. "They invest in a diversified portfolio of assets, including domestic infrastructure, global equities, and alternative investments, to mitigate risks and maximize returns."

The story then transitioned to a roundtable discussion where resource ministers from various countries shared their experiences and lessons learned from managing Sovereign Wealth Funds. Minister Lumamba shared Zambia's perspective and outlined the government's commitment to responsible resource management.

"Sovereign Wealth Funds play a crucial role in ensuring that resource wealth translates into lasting benefits for our citizens," Minister Lumamba stated during the discussion. "We are committed to establishing a transparent and accountable Sovereign Wealth Fund that supports our national development objectives and safeguards against volatility in commodity prices."

The narrative shifted to bilateral meetings where Minister Lumamba and Dr. Ng'andu engaged in discussions with investment managers and financial institutions interested in partnering with Zambia on its Sovereign Wealth Fund. They explored opportunities for collaboration and addressed investors' concerns about governance frameworks and investment strategies.

"Zambia presents attractive opportunities for responsible investment in natural resources," Minister Lumamba assured the investors during the meetings. "We are committed to partnering with reputable institutions to ensure that our Sovereign Wealth Fund generates sustainable returns and contributes to our long-term prosperity."

Back at the summit venue, Minister Lumamba and Dr. Ng'andu reflected on the day's discussions and insights. The atmosphere was one of optimism and determination as they prepared to return to Zambia and continue their efforts to establish a Sovereign Wealth Fund that would safeguard the country's natural resource wealth for future generations.

"As stewards of our natural resources, we have a responsibility to manage them wisely and ensure that they benefit all Zambians," Minister Lumamba concluded. "By harnessing the potential of Sovereign Wealth Funds, we can build a more prosperous and sustainable future for our nation."

The summit ended with a renewed sense of purpose, as delegates departed with a shared commitment to responsible resource management and the prudent use of Sovereign Wealth Funds to promote economic development and social progress.

8.5 Global Economic Crises and Contagion Effects

Minister of Finance Peter Lumamba, accompanied by his economic policy advisor, Mr. Joseph Chileshe, entered the bustling halls of the International Economic Forum in New York City. The air was filled with anticipation as delegates from around the world gathered to discuss the looming specter of global economic crises and contagion effects.

CHAPTER 8: PUBLIC FINANCE IN GLOBAL CONTEXT

"Welcome, Minister Lumamba, to the International Economic Forum," greeted the forum organizer as they entered the conference room. "Today, we examine the interconnectedness of the global economy and the potential contagion effects of economic crises."

Minister Lumamba stepped onto the stage, his presence commanding attention as he addressed the audience of policymakers, economists, and financial experts.

"Ladies and gentlemen, the global economy is at a crossroads," Minister Lumamba began, his voice resonating with urgency. "As we navigate the complexities of an interconnected world, we must remain vigilant against the threat of economic crises and contagion effects."

The setting transitioned to an expert panel discussion featuring leading economists and central bank governors. They engaged in a dynamic dialogue on the factors driving global economic crises and the potential spillover effects on vulnerable economies.

"Global economic crises can originate from various sources, including financial market disruptions, trade tensions, and geopolitical instability," remarked a renowned economist. "Their contagion effects can spread rapidly across borders, amplifying the impact on emerging and developing economies."

The narrative shifted to a case study presentation on past global economic crises and their contagion effects. The presenter highlighted the transmission channels through which crises spread, including trade linkages, financial market interconnections, and investor sentiment.

"The interconnectedness of the global economy has increased the speed and scale of contagion effects," explained the presenter. "During times of crisis, risk aversion rises, capital flows reverse, and vulnerable economies experience currency depreciation, capital flight, and declining investor confidence."

The story then transitioned to a roundtable discussion where finance ministers from various countries shared their experiences and strategies for mitigating the impact of global economic crises. Minister Lumamba shared Zambia's perspective and outlined the government's efforts to build resilience and prepare for future shocks.

"Global economic crises pose significant challenges for emerging and developing economies," Minister Lumamba stated during the discussion. "We are focused on strengthening our macroeconomic fundamentals, enhancing financial regulation and supervision, and diversifying our economy to reduce vulnerability to external shocks."

The narrative shifted to bilateral meetings where Minister Lumamba and Mr. Chileshe engaged in discussions with representatives from international financial institutions. They explored avenues for collaboration and assistance in building capacity and resilience to withstand global economic crises.

"International financial institutions play a critical role in providing support and assistance to countries affected by economic crises," Minister Lumamba emphasized during the meetings. "We welcome their expertise and resources in helping Zambia navigate through challenging times and build a more resilient economy."

Back at the forum venue, Minister Lumamba and Mr. Chileshe reflected on the day's discussions and insights. The atmosphere was one of determination and solidarity as they prepared to return to Zambia and continue their efforts to strengthen the country's resilience to global economic crises.

"As we confront the uncertainties of the global economy, let us remain united in our resolve to build a more stable and inclusive economic order," Minister Lumamba concluded. "By working together and learning from each other's experiences, we can mitigate the impact of economic crises and foster sustainable growth and development for all."

The forum ended with a renewed sense of purpose, as delegates departed with a shared commitment to collective action and cooperation in addressing the challenges of global economic crises and contagion effects.

8.6; Fiscal Federalization and Subnational Governance in a Globalized Economy

Minister of Finance Peter Lumamba, accompanied by his governance advisor, Ms. Patricia Banda, entered the elegant halls of the International Conference on Subnational Governance in Geneva. Delegates from various countries had convened to discuss the implications of fiscal federalization in a globalized economy.

"Welcome, Minister Lumamba, to the International Conference on Subnational Governance," greeted the conference organizer as they entered the conference room. "Today, we explore the challenges and opportunities of fiscal federalization in the context of an increasingly interconnected world."

Minister Lumamba stepped onto the stage, his presence commanding attention as he addressed the audience of policymakers, academics, and local government officials.

"Ladies and gentlemen, in a globalized economy, the governance of fiscal affairs at the subnational level is more critical than ever," Minister Lumamba began, his voice resonating with authority. "As we decentralize fiscal responsibilities, we must ensure effective governance structures that promote accountability, transparency, and sustainable development."

The setting transitioned to an expert panel discussion featuring leading scholars and practitioners in subnational governance. They engaged in a dynamic dialogue on the implications of fiscal federalization for subnational entities in a globalized economy.

"Fiscal federalization can empower subnational governments to address local needs and promote economic development," remarked a renowned governance expert. "However, it also poses challenges related to revenue mobilization, intergovernmental coordination, and fiscal sustainability."

The narrative shifted to a case study presentation on successful models of fiscal federalization from around the world. The presenter highlighted the key principles that underpin effective subnational governance, including fiscal autonomy, intergovernmental cooperation, and citizen participation.

"Successful models of fiscal federalization prioritize fiscal discipline, accountability, and transparency," explained the presenter. "They provide subnational governments with sufficient resources and autonomy to deliver public services efficiently and respond to local priorities."

The story then transitioned to a roundtable discussion where subnational leaders shared their experiences and strategies for managing fiscal decentralization. Minister Lumamba shared Zambia's perspective and outlined the government's efforts to strengthen subnational governance structures.

"Effective subnational governance is essential for promoting inclusive growth and reducing regional disparities," Minister Lumamba stated during the discussion. "We are committed to empowering local authorities, enhancing fiscal transparency, and building capacity at the subnational level."

The narrative shifted to bilateral meetings where Minister Lumamba and Ms. Banda engaged in discussions with representatives from local government associations. They explored opportunities for collaboration and assistance in strengthening subnational governance and fiscal management.

"Local governments are key partners in advancing national development objectives," Minister Lumamba emphasized during the meetings. "We are committed to working closely with local authorities to address their needs and support their efforts to deliver services effectively to their communities."

Back at the conference venue, Minister Lumamba and Ms. Banda reflected on the day's discussions and insights. The atmosphere was one of collaboration and solidarity as they prepared to return to Zambia and continue their efforts to strengthen subnational governance in the context of a globalized economy.

"As we decentralize fiscal responsibilities, let us remain committed to building strong and accountable institutions at the subnational level," Minister Lumamba concluded. "By empowering local authorities and fostering intergovernmental cooperation, we can promote inclusive growth and sustainable development for all."

The conference ended with a renewed sense of purpose, as delegates departed with a shared commitment to advancing subnational governance in the face of the challenges and opportunities presented by fiscal federalization in a globalized economy.

9

Chapter 9: Trade and Technology

9.1 Digital Trade and E-Commerce Regulations

Minister of Finance Peter Lumamba, accompanied by his technology advisor, Mr. James Mulenga, entered the futuristic venue of the International Summit on Digital Trade in Silicon Valley. Delegates from across the globe had gathered to discuss the evolving landscape of digital trade and the need for harmonized e-commerce regulations.

"Welcome, Minister Lumamba, to the International Summit on Digital Trade," greeted the summit organizer as they entered the conference room. "Today, we delve into the opportunities and challenges of digital trade and e-commerce regulations in the digital age."

Minister Lumamba took the stage, his presence commanding attention as he addressed the audience of policymakers, tech entrepreneurs, and industry leaders.

"Ladies and gentlemen, in an era of digital transformation,

digital trade has become a cornerstone of global commerce," Minister Lumamba began, his voice resonating with enthusiasm. "As we embrace the opportunities of the digital economy, we must also address the regulatory challenges to ensure a level playing field and protect consumers."

The setting transitioned to an expert panel discussion featuring leading experts in digital trade and e-commerce regulations. They engaged in a dynamic dialogue on the implications of digitalization for trade and the need for agile regulatory frameworks.

"The growth of digital trade presents immense opportunities for businesses to reach new markets and consumers," remarked a renowned tech policy expert. "However, it also raises concerns about data privacy, cybersecurity, and intellectual property rights that must be addressed through effective regulation."

The narrative shifted to a case study presentation on successful approaches to e-commerce regulation from around the world. The presenter highlighted the key elements of these regulatory frameworks, including consumer protection measures, data localization requirements, and cross-border data flows.

"Effective e-commerce regulations balance the need to foster innovation and protect consumers," explained the presenter. "They provide clear rules for online transactions, address the challenges of digital taxation, and promote trust and confidence in digital markets."

The story then transitioned to a roundtable discussion where trade ministers from various countries shared their experiences and strategies for regulating digital trade. Minister Lumamba shared Zambia's perspective and outlined the government's efforts to promote digitalization while ensuring regulatory coherence.

"Digital trade is a key driver of economic growth and competitiveness," Minister Lumamba stated during the discussion. "We are committed to developing a comprehensive regulatory framework that supports innovation, facilitates cross-border trade, and protects the rights of consumers and businesses."

The narrative shifted to bilateral meetings where Minister Lumamba and Mr. Mulenga engaged in discussions with representatives from leading tech companies. They explored opportunities for collaboration and partnership in promoting digital trade and shaping e-commerce regulations.

"The tech industry plays a crucial role in driving digital innovation and expanding digital trade," Minister Lumamba emphasized during the meetings. "We welcome your expertise and engagement in shaping regulatory policies that foster a vibrant and inclusive digital economy."

Back at the summit venue, Minister Lumamba and Mr. Mulenga reflected on the day's discussions and insights. The atmosphere was one of optimism and collaboration as they prepared to return to Zambia and continue their efforts to harness the potential of digital trade for economic growth and development.

"As we navigate the complexities of digital trade, let us remain committed to fostering an enabling environment that promotes innovation, entrepreneurship, and inclusive growth," Minister Lumamba concluded. "By working together with stakeholders across sectors, we can unlock the full potential of the digital economy and create shared prosperity for all."

The summit ended with a renewed sense of purpose, as delegates departed with a shared commitment to advancing digital trade and e-commerce regulations in an increasingly interconnected and digitalized world.

9.2 Innovation Policies and Technological Development

Minister of Finance Peter Lumamba, accompanied by his innovation advisor, Dr. Grace Mwape, entered the prestigious venue of the International Innovation Forum in Tokyo. Delegates from around the world had convened to discuss innovation policies and the role of technological development in shaping global trade.

"Welcome, Minister Lumamba, to the International Innovation Forum," greeted the forum organizer as they entered the conference room. "Today, we explore the intersection of innovation and trade, and the policies needed to foster technological development in the digital age."

Minister Lumamba took the stage, his presence commanding attention as he addressed the audience of policymakers, entrepreneurs, and researchers.

"Ladies and gentlemen, innovation is the lifeblood of progress and prosperity," Minister Lumamba began, his voice resonating with conviction. "As we navigate the complexities of the global economy, we must prioritize policies that promote technological development and unleash the power of innovation to drive sustainable growth."

The setting transitioned to an expert panel discussion featuring leading experts in innovation policy and technological development. They engaged in a dynamic dialogue on the role of government policies in fostering innovation and supporting entrepreneurship.

"Innovation policies play a crucial role in creating an environment conducive to technological development and economic diversification," remarked a renowned innovation strategist. "They should focus on promoting research and development, facilitating technology transfer, and fostering collaboration between academia, industry, and government."

The narrative shifted to a case study presentation on successful innovation policies from around the world. The presenter highlighted the key elements of these policies, including investment in education and skills development, support for startups and SMEs, and incentives for R&D investment.

"Successful innovation policies prioritize long-term investment in human capital and infrastructure," explained the presenter. "They create a supportive ecosystem that encourages experimentation, risk-taking, and the commercialization of new ideas."

The story then transitioned to a roundtable discussion where innovation ministers from various countries shared their experiences and strategies for promoting technological development. Minister Lumamba shared Zambia's perspective and outlined the government's efforts to foster innovation-driven growth.

"Innovation is a key driver of competitiveness and productivity in the global economy," Minister Lumamba stated during the discussion. "We are committed to developing a comprehensive innovation policy framework that harnesses the potential of our talented youth and fosters a culture of entrepreneurship and creativity."

The narrative shifted to bilateral meetings where Minister Lumamba and Dr. Mwape engaged in discussions with tech entrepreneurs and innovators. They explored opportunities for collaboration and partnership in advancing technological development and driving economic transformation.

"Tech entrepreneurs are at the forefront of innovation and job creation," Minister Lumamba emphasized during the meetings. "We are committed to supporting your efforts through targeted policies and programs that provide access to finance, markets, and skills training."

Back at the forum venue, Minister Lumamba and Dr. Mwape reflected on the day's discussions and insights. The atmosphere was one of excitement and determination as they prepared to return to Zambia and continue their efforts to promote innovation-driven growth and development.

"As we embrace the opportunities of the digital age, let us harness the power of innovation to address our most pressing challenges and build a better future for all," Minister Lumamba concluded. "By investing in innovation policies and fostering a culture of creativity and entrepreneurship, we can unlock new opportunities for economic prosperity and social progress."

The forum ended with a renewed sense of purpose, as delegates departed with a shared commitment to advancing innovation policies and technological development as drivers of inclusive and sustainable growth in the global economy.

9.3 Trade in Services and Mode 4 Movement of Persons

Minister of Finance Peter Lumamba, alongside his trade advisor, Dr. Sarah Banda, entered the bustling venue of the Global Services Trade Conference in Geneva. Delegates from various nations had convened to explore the nuances of trade in services and the movement of persons.

"Welcome, Minister Lumamba, to the Global Services Trade Conference," greeted the conference organizer as they entered the conference room. "Today, we delve into the complexities of services trade and the significance of Mode 4 movement of persons in the global economy."

Minister Lumamba ascended the stage, his presence commanding attention as he addressed the diverse audience of policymakers, industry leaders, and academics.

"Ladies and gentlemen, in an interconnected world, services trade plays a pivotal role in driving economic growth and enhancing global competitiveness," Minister Lumamba began, his voice resonating with authority. "As we navigate the intricacies of trade in services, we must recognize the importance of Mode 4 movement of persons in facilitating the cross-border exchange of skills, expertise, and innovation."

The setting transitioned to an expert panel discussion featuring leading experts in services trade and labor mobility. They engaged in a dynamic dialogue on the opportunities and challenges of Mode 4 movement of persons and its impact on economic development.

"Mode 4 movement of persons enables the temporary or permanent migration of individuals to provide services across borders," remarked a renowned trade economist. "It facilitates the transfer of knowledge, promotes cultural exchange, and fosters innovation and economic diversification."

The narrative shifted to a case study presentation highlighting successful examples of Mode 4 movement of persons from around the world. The presenter showcased instances where skilled professionals had contributed to the growth and competitiveness of industries in host countries.

"Mode 4 movement of persons benefits both sending and receiving countries by filling skill gaps, promoting technology transfer, and enhancing productivity," explained the presenter.

"However, it requires effective regulation and governance mechanisms to ensure the protection of workers' rights and the integrity of labor markets."

The story then transitioned to a roundtable discussion where trade ministers shared their experiences and perspectives on Mode 4 movement of persons. Minister Lumamba articulated Zambia's stance and outlined the government's efforts to leverage labor mobility for economic development.

"Mode 4 movement of persons presents significant opportunities for Zambia to tap into global talent pools and address skills shortages in key sectors," Minister Lumamba stated during the discussion. "We are committed to developing a regulatory framework that balances the needs of employers and workers while maximizing the benefits of labor mobility."

The narrative shifted to bilateral meetings where Minister Lumamba and Dr. Banda engaged in discussions with industry representatives from various service sectors. They explored opportunities for collaboration and partnership in leveraging Mode 4 movement of persons to drive innovation and competitiveness.

"Mode 4 movement of persons is integral to the growth and sustainability of our industry," emphasized a representative from the IT sector. "We welcome initiatives that facilitate the cross-border mobility of skilled professionals and promote the exchange of knowledge and expertise."

Back at the conference venue, Minister Lumamba and Dr. Banda reflected on the day's discussions and insights. The atmosphere was one of optimism and collaboration as they prepared to return to Zambia and continue their efforts to harness the potential of Mode 4 movement of persons for economic development.

"As we embrace the opportunities of services trade, let us remain committed to promoting inclusive growth and sustainable development through labor mobility," Minister Lumamba concluded. "By fostering a conducive environment for skilled professionals to contribute their talents, we can unlock new avenues for economic prosperity and global cooperation."

The conference ended with a renewed sense of purpose, as delegates departed with a shared commitment to advancing services trade and labor mobility as drivers of economic growth and human development.

9.4 Intellectual Property Rights (IPR) Protection and Enforcement

Minister of Finance Peter Lumamba, accompanied by his legal advisor, Ms. Alice Mulenga, entered the prestigious venue of the International Intellectual Property Rights Summit in London. Delegates from around the world had gathered to delve into the intricacies of intellectual property rights (IPR) protection and enforcement.

"Welcome, Minister Lumamba, to the International Intellectual Property Rights Summit," greeted the summit organizer as they entered the conference room. "Today, we explore the critical importance of IPR protection and enforcement in fostering innovation, creativity, and economic development."

Minister Lumamba took the stage, his presence commanding attention as he addressed the audience of policymakers, legal experts, and industry leaders.

"Ladies and gentlemen, intellectual property rights are the bedrock of innovation and creativity," Minister Lumamba began, his voice resonating with conviction. "As we navigate the complexities of the global economy, we must prioritize policies that safeguard intellectual property and encourage innovation-driven growth."

The setting transitioned to an expert panel discussion featuring leading experts in intellectual property law and enforcement. They engaged in a dynamic dialogue on the challenges and opportunities of IPR protection and the role of enforcement mechanisms in safeguarding innovation.

"Effective IPR protection is essential for incentivizing investment in research and development and promoting the commercialization of new ideas," remarked a renowned intellectual property lawyer. "However, it requires robust enforcement mechanisms to deter infringement and ensure the integrity of the innovation ecosystem."

The narrative shifted to a case study presentation highlighting successful examples of IPR protection and enforcement from around the world. The presenter showcased instances where strong legal frameworks and enforcement measures had facilitated technology transfer, attracted foreign investment, and promoted economic growth.

"Successful IPR protection and enforcement regimes strike a balance between the interests of rights holders, innovators, and consumers," explained the presenter. "They provide legal certainty, promote fair competition, and incentivize innovation while safeguarding public health, safety, and welfare."

The story then transitioned to a roundtable discussion where trade ministers shared their experiences and strategies for enhancing IPR protection and enforcement in their respective countries. Minister Lumamba articulated Zambia's commitment to strengthening its legal framework and enforcement mechanisms.

"IPR protection and enforcement are integral to Zambia's efforts to promote innovation-driven growth and attract investment," Minister Lumamba stated during the discussion. "We are committed to enhancing our legal framework, building institutional capacity, and fostering collaboration with stakeholders to combat piracy and counterfeiting."

The narrative shifted to bilateral meetings where Minister Lumamba and Ms. Mulenga engaged in discussions with industry representatives from various sectors. They explored opportunities for collaboration and partnership in promoting IPR protection and enforcement to drive innovation and competitiveness.

"Strong IPR protection is critical for fostering a conducive environment for innovation and investment," emphasized a representative from the pharmaceutical industry. "We welcome initiatives that strengthen legal frameworks and enforcement mechanisms to safeguard intellectual property and incentivize research and development."

Back at the summit venue, Minister Lumamba and Ms. Mulenga reflected on the day's discussions and insights. The atmosphere was one of determination and collaboration as they prepared to return to Zambia and continue their efforts to strengthen IPR protection and enforcement.

"As we safeguard intellectual property rights, let us remain steadfast in our commitment to promoting innovation, creativity, and economic development," Minister Lumamba concluded. "By fostering a culture of respect for intellectual property and investing in enforcement measures, we can unlock the full potential of our knowledge economy and create a better future for all."

The summit ended with a renewed sense of purpose, as delegates departed with a shared commitment to advancing IPR protection and enforcement as drivers of innovation, growth, and prosperity.

9.5 Artificial Intelligence (AI) and the Future of Trade

Minister of Finance Peter Lumamba, accompanied by his technology advisor, Mr. James Mulenga, entered the state-of-the-art venue of the Global Artificial Intelligence Summit in Beijing. Delegates from across the world had convened to explore the transformative potential of artificial intelligence (AI) in shaping the future of trade.

"Welcome, Minister Lumamba, to the Global Artificial Intelligence Summit," greeted the summit organizer as they entered the conference room. "Today, we delve into the profound impact of AI on trade and the opportunities and challenges it presents for global commerce."

Minister Lumamba took the stage, his presence commanding attention as he addressed the audience of policymakers, tech leaders, and industry experts.

"Ladies and gentlemen, artificial intelligence is revolutionizing every aspect of our lives, including the way we trade," Minister Lumamba began, his voice resonating with anticipation. "As we stand on the cusp of the AI revolution, we must embrace its potential to drive innovation, enhance productivity, and reshape global trade patterns."

The setting transitioned to an expert panel discussion featuring leading experts in AI technology and trade policy. They engaged in a dynamic dialogue on the implications of AI for trade, including its role in automating processes, optimizing supply chains, and facilitating cross-border transactions.

"AI technologies, such as machine learning and natural language processing, have the potential to revolutionize trade by streamlining processes, reducing costs, and enabling predictive analytics," remarked a renowned AI researcher. "However, they also raise concerns about job displacement, data privacy, and algorithmic bias that must be addressed through responsible governance frameworks."

The narrative shifted to a case study presentation highlighting successful applications of AI in trade from around the world. The presenter showcased examples where AI-powered solutions had improved efficiency, accuracy, and decision-making across various sectors, from logistics and finance to e-commerce and market analysis.

"AI-driven innovations, such as smart contracts, virtual assistants, and predictive analytics, are transforming the way we conduct trade," explained the presenter. "They have the potential to unlock new opportunities for businesses, increase market access, and drive inclusive growth and development."

The story then transitioned to a roundtable discussion where trade ministers shared their perspectives on the opportunities and challenges of AI for trade policy. Minister Lumamba articulated Zambia's vision for leveraging AI to enhance its competitiveness and expand its global footprint.

"AI is a game-changer for trade, and Zambia is committed to harnessing its potential to drive economic growth and prosperity," Minister Lumamba stated during the discussion. "We recognize the need for proactive policies that promote innovation, protect intellectual property, and ensure ethical AI deployment."

The narrative shifted to bilateral meetings where Minister

Lumamba and Mr. Mulenga engaged in discussions with AI innovators and entrepreneurs. They explored opportunities for collaboration and partnership in developing AI-driven solutions to address trade-related challenges and opportunities.

"AI technologies have the power to revolutionize global trade by unlocking new insights, optimizing processes, and facilitating smarter decision-making," emphasized a representative from a tech startup. "We welcome partnerships with governments and businesses to co-create AI solutions that drive sustainable and inclusive trade."

Back at the summit venue, Minister Lumamba and Mr. Mulenga reflected on the day's discussions and insights. The atmosphere was one of excitement and anticipation as they prepared to return to Zambia and continue their efforts to embrace AI as a catalyst for trade innovation and growth.

"As we embark on the AI revolution, let us remain vigilant in addressing its ethical, social, and economic implications," Minister Lumamba concluded. "By fostering collaboration, investing in skills development, and promoting responsible AI governance, we can harness the transformative power of AI to build a more prosperous and inclusive future for all."

The summit ended with a renewed sense of purpose, as delegates departed with a shared commitment to advancing AI-driven innovation as a driver of sustainable trade and economic development.

9.6 Blockchain Technology and Trade Finance Innovation

Minister of Finance Peter Lumamba, accompanied by his financial advisor, Mr. David Banda, entered the bustling venue of the International Blockchain Technology Expo in New York City. Delegates from around the world had gathered to explore the transformative potential of blockchain technology in revolutionizing trade finance.

"Welcome, Minister Lumamba, to the International Blockchain Technology Expo," greeted the expo organizer as they entered the exhibition hall. "Today, we delve into the innovative applications of blockchain technology in trade finance and the opportunities it presents for enhancing transparency, efficiency, and inclusivity in global trade."

Minister Lumamba took the stage, his presence commanding attention as he addressed the audience of policymakers, financial experts, and industry leaders.

"Ladies and gentlemen, blockchain technology holds the promise of transforming trade finance by providing secure, transparent, and efficient solutions for managing and financing cross-border transactions," Minister Lumamba began, his voice resonating with enthusiasm. "As we stand at the forefront of the blockchain revolution, we must harness its potential to unlock new opportunities for trade and economic development."

The setting transitioned to an expert panel discussion featuring leading experts in blockchain technology and trade finance. They engaged in a dynamic dialogue on the transformative impact of blockchain on trade finance processes, including letter of credit issuance, supply chain financing, and trade documentation.

"Blockchain technology offers unprecedented levels of security, transparency, and efficiency in trade finance," remarked a renowned blockchain strategist. "By enabling real-time data sharing, automated contract execution, and immutable record-keeping, it has the potential to streamline trade processes, reduce costs, and mitigate risks for all stakeholders."

The narrative shifted to a case study presentation highlighting successful applications of blockchain in trade finance from around the world. The presenter showcased examples where blockchain-based platforms had facilitated faster, more secure, and cost-effective trade transactions, benefiting exporters, importers, and financial institutions alike.

"Blockchain technology is revolutionizing trade finance by eliminating intermediaries, reducing transaction times, and enhancing trust and transparency in cross-border transactions," explained the presenter. "It has the potential to unlock trillions of dollars in trapped capital, particularly for small and medium-sized enterprises (SMEs) that face challenges in accessing traditional financing."

The story then transitioned to a roundtable discussion where trade ministers shared their perspectives on the opportunities and challenges of blockchain for trade finance innovation. Minister Lumamba articulated Zambia's commitment to leveraging blockchain to enhance its trade competitiveness and support SMEs.

"Blockchain technology has the potential to democratize access to trade finance and empower SMEs to participate more actively in global trade," Minister Lumamba stated during the discussion. "We recognize the need for collaborative efforts to develop regulatory frameworks, build capacity, and foster innovation in blockchain-based solutions for trade finance."

The narrative shifted to bilateral meetings where Minister Lumamba and Mr. Banda engaged in discussions with FinTech entrepreneurs and innovators. They explored opportunities for collaboration and partnership in developing blockchain-based solutions to address trade finance challenges and enhance financial inclusion.

"Blockchain technology has the power to revolutionize trade finance by reducing costs, increasing transparency, and expanding access to financing for SMEs," emphasized a representative from a blockchain startup. "We welcome partnerships with governments and financial institutions to drive innovation and promote inclusive growth."

Back at the expo venue, Minister Lumamba and Mr. Banda reflected on the day's discussions and insights. The atmosphere was one of excitement and optimism as they prepared to return to Zambia and continue their efforts to embrace blockchain as a catalyst for trade finance innovation and economic development.

"As we embrace the transformative potential of blockchain technology, let us remain committed to fostering an enabling environment for innovation, collaboration, and inclusive growth," Minister Lumamba concluded. "By harnessing blockchain to revolutionize trade finance, we can unlock new opportunities for businesses, promote financial inclusion, and drive sustainable economic development."

The expo ended with a renewed sense of purpose, as delegates departed with a shared commitment to advancing blockchain-based solutions as drivers of trade finance innovation and global trade expansion.

10

Chapter 10: Regional Economic Integration Models and Lessons

10.1 European Union (EU) Integration Models and Lessons Learned

Minister of Finance Peter Lumamba, accompanied by his economic advisor, Dr. Sarah Mwansa, entered the prestigious venue of the International Economic Integration Conference in Brussels. Delegates from around the world had gathered to explore regional economic integration models and the lessons they offered for fostering cooperation and growth.

"Welcome, Minister Lumamba, to the International Economic Integration Conference," greeted the conference organizer as they entered the conference room. "Today, we delve into the diverse experiences of regional economic integration, with a focus on the European Union (EU) and the valuable lessons it provides for other regions."

Minister Lumamba took the stage, his presence commanding attention as he addressed the audience of policymakers, economists, and diplomats.

"Ladies and gentlemen, regional economic integration is a powerful force for promoting peace, stability, and prosperity," Minister Lumamba began, his voice resonating with conviction. "As we examine the EU integration models and lessons learned, we gain valuable insights into the challenges and opportunities of fostering economic cooperation and convergence among diverse nations."

The setting transitioned to an expert panel discussion featuring leading experts in regional economic integration and EU studies. They engaged in a dynamic dialogue on the evolution of the EU integration process, its institutional framework, and the economic benefits and challenges experienced by member states.

"The EU integration experience demonstrates the transformative power of economic integration in promoting trade, investment, and economic convergence among member states," remarked a renowned EU economist. "However, it also highlights the importance of addressing disparities, promoting inclusive growth, and strengthening institutional mechanisms to ensure the sustainability of integration efforts."

The narrative shifted to a case study presentation highlighting key milestones and challenges in the EU integration process. The presenter showcased examples of successful integration initiatives, such as the single market, the euro currency, and the Schengen area, and analyzed their impact on trade, investment, and economic development.

"The EU integration process has been characterized by bold vision, political commitment, and gradual steps towards deeper economic and political union," explained the presenter. "It has brought significant economic benefits to member states, including increased trade flows, higher productivity, and enhanced competitiveness in global markets."

The story then transitioned to a roundtable discussion where trade ministers shared their perspectives on the EU integration models and their relevance for other regions. Minister Lumamba articulated Zambia's interest in exploring regional economic integration as a means of promoting trade, investment, and development.

"The EU integration experience offers valuable lessons for regions seeking to enhance economic cooperation and integration," Minister Lumamba stated during the discussion. "We recognize the need for inclusive, sustainable integration models that prioritize the interests of all member states and address the unique challenges they face."

The narrative shifted to bilateral meetings where Minister Lumamba and Dr. Mwansa engaged in discussions with EU representatives and experts. They explored opportunities for collaboration and knowledge sharing in the areas of regional economic integration, trade policy, and institutional capacity building.

"The EU remains committed to supporting the integration efforts of partner regions and sharing its experiences and best practices," emphasized a representative from the European Commission. "We welcome partnerships with countries like Zambia to promote economic cooperation, trade facilitation, and sustainable development."

Back at the conference venue, Minister Lumamba and Dr. Mwansa reflected on the day's discussions and insights. The atmosphere was one of inspiration and collaboration as they prepared to return to Zambia and continue their efforts to promote regional economic integration as a catalyst for growth and development.

"As we draw lessons from the EU integration experience, let us remain committed to fostering cooperation, dialogue, and partnership among nations," Minister Lumamba concluded. "By learning from each other and working together, we can build a more prosperous, inclusive, and resilient global economy."

The conference ended with a renewed sense of purpose, as delegates departed with a shared commitment to advancing regional economic integration as a pathway to sustainable development and shared prosperity.

10.2 African Continental Free Trade Area (AfCFTA) Implementation

Minister of Finance Peter Lumamba, accompanied by his trade advisor, Mr. Joseph Lungu, entered the vibrant venue of the African Continental Free Trade Area (AfCFTA) Summit in Addis Ababa. Leaders and delegates from across Africa had gathered to discuss the implementation of the historic trade agreement.

"Welcome, Minister Lumamba, to the AfCFTA Summit," greeted the summit organizer as they entered the conference hall. "Today, we gather to accelerate the implementation of the AfCFTA and unlock the economic potential of the African continent."

Minister Lumamba ascended the stage, his presence commanding attention as he addressed the audience of African leaders, policymakers, and business representatives.

"Ladies and gentlemen, the AfCFTA represents a historic

opportunity to unleash Africa's economic potential and foster inclusive growth and development," Minister Lumamba began, his voice resonating with passion. "As we embark on this transformative journey, let us draw inspiration from the successes and challenges of regional economic integration efforts around the world."

The setting transitioned to an expert panel discussion featuring leading experts in trade policy and African integration. They engaged in a dynamic dialogue on the opportunities and challenges of implementing the AfCFTA, including trade facilitation, infrastructure development, and regulatory harmonization.

"The AfCFTA has the potential to boost intra-African trade, create jobs, and stimulate industrialization and economic diversification," remarked a renowned African economist. "However, its successful implementation requires coordinated efforts to address infrastructure constraints, trade barriers, and capacity gaps across member states."

The narrative shifted to a case study presentation highlighting successful examples of regional economic integration in Africa. The presenter showcased instances where regional trade agreements and customs unions had led to increased trade flows, investment, and economic growth among member states.

"Regional economic integration initiatives in Africa have demonstrated the benefits of closer economic cooperation and trade liberalization," explained the presenter. "They have facilitated cross-border trade, enhanced competitiveness, and promoted regional value chains, laying the groundwork for the AfCFTA's success."

The story then transitioned to a roundtable discussion

where African trade ministers shared their perspectives on the implementation of the AfCFTA and the priorities for advancing regional economic integration. Minister Lumamba articulated Zambia's commitment to supporting the AfCFTA and promoting trade facilitation measures.

"The AfCFTA represents a historic opportunity to create a single market for goods and services, expand intra-African trade, and boost economic growth and development," Minister Lumamba stated during the discussion. "We must prioritize efforts to address infrastructure deficits, streamline customs procedures, and enhance regulatory harmonization to maximize the benefits of the AfCFTA for all African countries."

The narrative shifted to bilateral meetings where Minister Lumamba and Mr. Lungu engaged in discussions with African leaders and representatives. They explored opportunities for collaboration and partnership in advancing the AfCFTA agenda and addressing key challenges facing African economies.

"The AfCFTA is a game-changer for Africa's economic transformation," emphasized a representative from a neighboring country. "We welcome Zambia's leadership in driving the implementation of the AfCFTA and look forward to working together to unlock its full potential for the benefit of our people."

Back at the summit venue, Minister Lumamba and Mr. Lungu reflected on the day's discussions and insights. The atmosphere was one of optimism and determination as they prepared to return to Zambia and continue their efforts to support the implementation of the AfCFTA.

"As we move forward with the AfCFTA, let us remain committed to overcoming challenges, fostering cooperation, and seizing the opportunities for shared prosperity and development," Minister Lumamba concluded. "By working together, we can build a more integrated, resilient, and prosperous Africa for future generations."

The AfCFTA Summit ended with a renewed sense of unity and purpose, as African leaders departed with a shared commitment to advancing regional economic integration as a catalyst for sustainable development and prosperity on the continent.

10.3 Asia-Pacific Economic Cooperation (APEC) and Regional Cooperation

Minister of Finance Peter Lumamba, accompanied by his international relations advisor, Ms. Grace Tembo, entered the bustling venue of the Asia-Pacific Economic Cooperation (APEC) Summit in Tokyo. Leaders and delegates from across the Asia-Pacific region had gathered to discuss regional cooperation and economic integration.

"Welcome, Minister Lumamba, to the APEC Summit," greeted the summit organizer as they entered the conference hall. "Today, we convene to strengthen cooperation and promote economic integration across the Asia-Pacific region."

Minister Lumamba took the stage, his presence commanding attention as he addressed the audience of regional leaders, policymakers, and business executives.

"Ladies and gentlemen, the Asia-Pacific region is a powerhouse of economic dynamism and innovation," Minister Lumamba began, his voice resonating with conviction. "As we navigate the complex challenges of the 21st century, let us harness the spirit of cooperation and solidarity to promote inclusive growth and sustainable development."

The setting transitioned to an expert panel discussion featuring leading experts in regional cooperation and economic integration. They engaged in a dynamic dialogue on the opportunities and challenges of fostering collaboration among APEC member economies, including trade liberalization, digital innovation, and sustainable development.

"APEC has played a crucial role in promoting economic integration and cooperation across the Asia-Pacific region," remarked a renowned regional economist. "Through initiatives such as the Bogor Goals and the APEC Business Travel Card, APEC has facilitated trade liberalization, investment promotion, and capacity building among member economies."

The narrative shifted to a case study presentation highlighting successful examples of regional cooperation and economic integration within the APEC framework. The presenter showcased instances where APEC initiatives had led to increased trade flows, technology transfer, and infrastructure development across member economies.

"APEC's collaborative approach to addressing common challenges and seizing shared opportunities has yielded tangible benefits for the Asia-Pacific region," explained the presenter. "From fostering innovation and entrepreneurship to promoting sustainable development and connectivity, APEC has been instrumental in driving regional economic growth and prosperity."

The story then transitioned to a roundtable discussion where APEC leaders shared their perspectives on the importance of regional cooperation and the priorities for advancing economic integration. Minister Lumamba articulated Zambia's interest in strengthening its engagement with APEC and promoting trade and investment linkages with Asia-Pacific economies.

CHAPTER 10: REGIONAL ECONOMIC INTEGRATION MODELS AND LESSONS

"The Asia-Pacific region is a key driver of global economic growth and innovation," Minister Lumamba stated during the discussion. "We recognize the strategic importance of deepening our cooperation with APEC economies to unlock new opportunities for trade, investment, and sustainable development."

The narrative shifted to bilateral meetings where Minister Lumamba and Ms. Tembo engaged in discussions with APEC representatives and delegates. They explored opportunities for collaboration and partnership in areas such as trade facilitation, digital economy, and green growth.

"APEC remains committed to promoting open, transparent, and rules-based trade and investment in the Asia-Pacific region," emphasized a representative from an APEC member economy. "We welcome Zambia's interest in enhancing its engagement with APEC and look forward to exploring new avenues for cooperation and partnership."

Back at the summit venue, Minister Lumamba and Ms. Tembo reflected on the day's discussions and insights. The atmosphere was one of optimism and collaboration as they prepared to return to Zambia and continue their efforts to deepen regional cooperation and economic integration.

"As we strengthen our engagement with APEC, let us seize the opportunities for mutual benefit and shared prosperity," Minister Lumamba concluded. "By fostering dialogue, building trust, and promoting inclusive growth, we can create a more resilient and interconnected Asia-Pacific community."

The APEC Summit ended with a renewed commitment to advancing regional cooperation and economic integration as drivers of sustainable development and prosperity in the Asia-Pacific region.

10.4 Mercosur and South American Integration Efforts

Minister of Finance Peter Lumamba, accompanied by his diplomatic advisor, Mr. Elias Mwape, arrived at the Mercosur headquarters in Montevideo. Leaders and delegates from South American countries had gathered to discuss regional integration efforts and the role of Mercosur in fostering economic cooperation.

"Welcome, Minister Lumamba, to Mercosur," greeted the summit organizer as they entered the conference room. "Today, we convene to strengthen our ties and promote integration among South American countries."

Minister Lumamba took the stage, his presence commanding attention as he addressed the audience of South American leaders, policymakers, and diplomats.

"Ladies and gentlemen, Mercosur stands as a beacon of regional integration and cooperation in South America," Minister Lumamba began, his voice resonating with admiration. "As we gather to reaffirm our commitment to Mercosur, let us explore ways to deepen our economic ties and promote shared prosperity."

The setting transitioned to an expert panel discussion featuring leading experts in regional integration and Mercosur studies. They engaged in a dynamic dialogue on the opportunities and challenges of fostering economic cooperation among Mercosur member countries, including trade liberalization, infrastructure development, and regulatory harmonization.

"Mercosur has made significant strides in promoting economic integration and cooperation among South American countries," remarked a renowned regional economist. "Through initiatives such as the Common Market, Mercosur

CHAPTER 10: REGIONAL ECONOMIC INTEGRATION MODELS AND LESSONS

has facilitated trade liberalization, investment promotion, and economic convergence among member states."

The narrative shifted to a case study presentation highlighting successful examples of regional integration within Mercosur. The presenter showcased instances where Mercosur initiatives had led to increased trade flows, investment, and economic growth among member countries.

"Mercosur's commitment to fostering economic cooperation and integration has yielded tangible benefits for South American countries," explained the presenter. "From promoting regional trade and investment to enhancing infrastructure connectivity and facilitating labor mobility, Mercosur has played a vital role in driving economic development and integration in the region."

The story then transitioned to a roundtable discussion where Mercosur leaders shared their perspectives on the importance of regional integration and the priorities for advancing economic cooperation. Minister Lumamba articulated Zambia's interest in strengthening its ties with Mercosur and exploring opportunities for trade and investment cooperation.

"Mercosur remains committed to promoting economic integration and cooperation among South American countries," Minister Lumamba stated during the discussion. "We recognize the strategic importance of deepening our engagement with Mercosur and look forward to exploring new avenues for collaboration and partnership."

The narrative shifted to bilateral meetings where Minister Lumamba and Mr. Mwape engaged in discussions with Mercosur representatives and delegates. They explored opportunities for collaboration and partnership in areas such as trade facilitation, infrastructure development, and energy cooperation.

"Mercosur welcomes Zambia's interest in strengthening its ties with South American countries," emphasized a representative from Mercosur. "We believe that enhanced cooperation and integration will benefit all member countries and contribute to the economic development and prosperity of the region."

Back at the Mercosur headquarters, Minister Lumamba and Mr. Mwape reflected on the day's discussions and insights. The atmosphere was one of optimism and collaboration as they prepared to return to Zambia and continue their efforts to deepen regional integration and economic cooperation.

"As we strengthen our ties with Mercosur, let us seize the opportunities for mutual benefit and shared prosperity," Minister Lumamba concluded. "By fostering dialogue, building trust, and promoting inclusive growth, we can create a more integrated and prosperous South America."

The meeting ended with a renewed commitment to advancing regional integration and economic cooperation as drivers of sustainable development and prosperity in South America.

10.5 Economic Community of West African States (ECOWAS) Regional Integration

Minister of Finance Peter Lumamba, accompanied by his economic advisor, Mrs. Patricia Ngoma, arrived at the headquarters of the Economic Community of West African States (ECOWAS) in Abuja. Leaders and delegates from West African countries had gathered to discuss regional integration efforts and the role of ECOWAS in fostering economic cooperation.

"Welcome, Minister Lumamba, to ECOWAS," greeted the

CHAPTER 10: REGIONAL ECONOMIC INTEGRATION MODELS AND LESSONS

summit organizer as they entered the conference room. "Today, we convene to strengthen our ties and promote integration among West African countries."

Minister Lumamba took the stage, his presence commanding attention as he addressed the audience of West African leaders, policymakers, and diplomats.

"Ladies and gentlemen, ECOWAS is a pillar of regional integration and cooperation in West Africa," Minister Lumamba began, his voice resonating with determination. "As we gather to reaffirm our commitment to ECOWAS, let us explore ways to deepen our economic ties and promote shared prosperity."

The setting transitioned to an expert panel discussion featuring leading experts in regional integration and ECOWAS studies. They engaged in a dynamic dialogue on the opportunities and challenges of fostering economic cooperation among ECOWAS member countries, including trade facilitation, infrastructure development, and institutional capacity building.

"ECOWAS has made significant strides in promoting economic integration and cooperation among West African countries," remarked a renowned regional economist. "Through initiatives such as the ECOWAS Trade Liberalization Scheme and the ECOWAS Common External Tariff, ECOWAS has facilitated trade liberalization, investment promotion, and economic convergence among member states."

The narrative shifted to a case study presentation highlighting successful examples of regional integration within ECOWAS. The presenter showcased instances where ECOWAS initiatives had led to increased trade flows, investment, and economic growth among member countries.

"ECOWAS's commitment to fostering economic cooperation and integration has yielded tangible benefits for West African countries," explained the presenter. "From promoting regional trade and investment to enhancing infrastructure connectivity and facilitating labor mobility, ECOWAS has played a vital role in driving economic development and integration in the region."

The story then transitioned to a roundtable discussion where ECOWAS leaders shared their perspectives on the importance of regional integration and the priorities for advancing economic cooperation. Minister Lumamba articulated Zambia's interest in strengthening its ties with ECOWAS and exploring opportunities for trade and investment cooperation.

"ECOWAS remains committed to promoting economic integration and cooperation among West African countries," Minister Lumamba stated during the discussion. "We recognize the strategic importance of deepening our engagement with ECOWAS and look forward to exploring new avenues for collaboration and partnership."

The narrative shifted to bilateral meetings where Minister Lumamba and Mrs. Ngoma engaged in discussions with ECOWAS representatives and delegates. They explored opportunities for collaboration and partnership in areas such as trade facilitation, infrastructure development, and energy cooperation.

"ECOWAS welcomes Zambia's interest in strengthening its ties with West African countries," emphasized a representative from ECOWAS. "We believe that enhanced cooperation and integration will benefit all member countries and contribute to the economic development and prosperity of the region."

Back at the ECOWAS headquarters, Minister Lumamba and Mrs. Ngoma reflected on the day's discussions and insights. The atmosphere was one of optimism and collaboration as they prepared to return to Zambia and continue their efforts to deepen regional integration and economic cooperation.

"As we strengthen our ties with ECOWAS, let us seize the opportunities for mutual benefit and shared prosperity," Minister Lumamba concluded. "By fostering dialogue, building trust, and promoting inclusive growth, we can create a more integrated and prosperous West Africa."

The meeting ended with a renewed commitment to advancing regional integration and economic cooperation as drivers of sustainable development and prosperity in West Africa.

10.6 Association of Southeast Asian Nations (ASEAN) Economic Integration Initiatives

Minister of Finance Peter Lumamba, accompanied by his trade advisor, Mr. Joseph Lungu, arrived at the ASEAN Secretariat in Jakarta. Leaders and delegates from Southeast Asian countries had gathered to discuss regional integration efforts and the role of ASEAN in fostering economic cooperation.

"Welcome, Minister Lumamba, to the ASEAN Secretariat," greeted the summit organizer as they entered the conference room. "Today, we convene to strengthen our ties and promote integration among Southeast Asian countries."

Minister Lumamba took the stage, his presence commanding attention as he addressed the audience of ASEAN leaders, policymakers, and diplomats.

"Ladies and gentlemen, ASEAN is a beacon of regional integration and cooperation in Southeast Asia," Minister Lumamba began, his voice resonating with determination. "As we gather to reaffirm our commitment to ASEAN, let us explore ways to deepen our economic ties and promote shared prosperity."

The setting transitioned to an expert panel discussion featuring leading experts in regional integration and ASEAN studies. They engaged in a dynamic dialogue on the opportunities and challenges of fostering economic cooperation among ASEAN member countries, including trade liberalization, infrastructure development, and institutional capacity building.

"ASEAN has made significant strides in promoting economic integration and cooperation among Southeast Asian countries," remarked a renowned regional economist. "Through initiatives such as the ASEAN Economic Community (AEC) Blueprint and the ASEAN Free Trade Area, ASEAN has facilitated trade liberalization, investment promotion, and economic convergence among member states."

The narrative shifted to a case study presentation highlighting successful examples of regional integration within ASEAN. The presenter showcased instances where ASEAN initiatives had led to increased trade flows, investment, and economic growth among member countries.

"ASEAN's commitment to fostering economic cooperation and integration has yielded tangible benefits for Southeast Asian countries," explained the presenter. "From promoting regional trade and investment to enhancing infrastructure connectivity and facilitating labor mobility, ASEAN has played a vital role in driving economic development and integration in the region."

The story then transitioned to a roundtable discussion where ASEAN leaders shared their perspectives on the importance of regional integration and the priorities for advancing economic cooperation. Minister Lumamba articulated Zambia's interest in strengthening its ties with ASEAN and exploring opportunities for trade and investment cooperation.

CHAPTER 10: REGIONAL ECONOMIC INTEGRATION MODELS AND LESSONS

"ASEAN remains committed to promoting economic integration and cooperation among Southeast Asian countries," Minister Lumamba stated during the discussion. "We recognize the strategic importance of deepening our engagement with ASEAN and look forward to exploring new avenues for collaboration and partnership."

The narrative shifted to bilateral meetings where Minister Lumamba and Mr. Lungu engaged in discussions with ASEAN representatives and delegates. They explored opportunities for collaboration and partnership in areas such as trade facilitation, infrastructure development, and digital innovation.

"ASEAN welcomes Zambia's interest in strengthening its ties with Southeast Asian countries," emphasized a representative from ASEAN. "We believe that enhanced cooperation and integration will benefit all member countries and contribute to the economic development and prosperity of the region."

Back at the ASEAN Secretariat, Minister Lumamba and Mr. Lungu reflected on the day's discussions and insights. The atmosphere was one of optimism and collaboration as they prepared to return to Zambia and continue their efforts to deepen regional integration and economic cooperation.

"As we strengthen our ties with ASEAN, let us seize the opportunities for mutual benefit and shared prosperity," Minister Lumamba concluded. "By fostering dialogue, building trust, and promoting inclusive growth, we can create a more integrated and prosperous Southeast Asia."

The meeting ended with a renewed commitment to advancing regional integration and economic cooperation as drivers of sustainable development and prosperity in Southeast Asia.

About the Author

Goodson Mumba is a multifaceted individual known for his diverse expertise and prolific contributions across various fields. As an infopreneur, thought leader, and spiritual leader, he has inspired countless individuals through his insightful teachings and impactful writings. Mumba is also an accomplished author, with several notable works to his name, including "Understanding Corporate Worship," "The Years I Spent in a Week," "Management By Harmony," "The CEO's Diary," "Change to Change" and "Creative Thinking for results" His literary works span topics ranging from business management to personal development and spirituality, reflecting his broad range of interests and insights.

With a Master of Business Leadership (MBL) and a Bachelor of Arts in Theology (BTh), Mumba brings a unique blend of business acumen and spiritual wisdom to his work. His educational background is further enriched by a Group Diploma in Management Studies, providing him with a solid foundation in organizational dynamics and leadership principles. Additionally, Mumba holds diplomas in Education Psychology,

Leadership and Management Styles, Organizational Behaviour, Financial Accounting, Economic Growth and Development, and Project Management, showcasing his commitment to continuous learning and professional development.

Mumba's expertise extends beyond traditional academic disciplines, encompassing areas such as Neuro-Linguistic Programming (NLP) and Positive Psychology. His diverse skill set is complemented by a range of certifications, including Creative Problem Solving and Decision Making, Life Coaching Fundamentals and Techniques, Professional Life Coaching, and Performance Management System Design. These certifications reflect Mumba's dedication to equipping himself with the tools and knowledge necessary to empower others and drive positive change.

As an author, Mumba's writings reflect his deep understanding of human nature, organizational dynamics, and spiritual principles. His works offer practical insights, actionable strategies, and inspirational guidance for individuals seeking personal growth, professional success, and spiritual fulfillment. Mumba's holistic approach to life and leadership resonates with readers worldwide, making him a respected figure in both the business and spiritual communities.

Overall, Goodson Mumba's diverse background, extensive knowledge, and profound insights make him a sought-after speaker, mentor, and author. His commitment to excellence, lifelong learning, and service to others continues to inspire individuals to unlock their full potential and lead lives of purpose and significance.

Goodson Mumba is renowned for initiating the concept of Management by Harmony, revolutionizing traditional management practices with a focus on balanced and holistic approaches. He has authored two influential books on this subject "Introduction to Management by Harmony" and its sequel, "Management by Harmony."

Mumba's work has significantly impacted the field, offering innovative strategies for fostering organizational harmony and efficiency. His contributions continue to shape contemporary management theories and practices.

www.ingramcontent.com/pod-product-compliance
Lightning Source LLC
Chambersburg PA
CBHW071830210526
45479CB00001B/66